French Tarts

French Tarts

BY
JO GOSLING

OCTOPUS BOOKS

Recipe Notes

Ovens should be preheated to the specified temperature.

All spoon measures are level.

Measurements are given in Metric, Imperial and American.
Follow one set of measurements only – they are not interchangeable.

All 20cm/8 inch savoury tarts serve 6 as a main course and 8 as a
starter. All 20cm/8 inch sweet tarts serve 6 to 8. The salads and
sauces serve 6 unless otherwise stated.

First published 1985 by
Octopus Books Limited
59 Grosvenor Street,
London W1

© 1985 Octopus Books Limited
ISBN 0 7064 2331 3

Produced by Mandarin Publishers Ltd
22a Westlands Road, Quarry Bay, Hong Kong

Printed in Hong Kong

Contents

In Defence of Tarts

If you are ever at a loss when it comes to entertaining, then this book should solve your problems. The introduction of a French Tart into a meal provides a definite conversation piece. The versatility of this species enables the cook to sneak one onto the table, under various guises, and be assured of compliments.
A tart looks impressive, tastes delightful and is simple to prepare.

A while ago I was fortunate enough to live and work in Normandy.
I made many longlasting friendships with cooks who generously introduced me to 'La Tarte Française', and passed on their personal recipes and tips.
Each friend had her own infallible way of making pastry; I therefore concluded that the methods are, to a large extent, interchangeable.

This collection of recipes demonstrates the wide range of possible ingredients for both sweet and savoury tarts. I have even included a section which is devoted solely to the apple tart. Even these ten apple recipes do not exhaust the possibilities, for with a little imagination the number of combinations can be infinite. Never be afraid to experiment with your tarts. If a main ingredient is unavailable then try another. You will probably surprise yourself with the result, *et voilà* you will have invented a new recipe.

I sincerely hope that you find this book as exciting to read as I did to write.
If it inspires you to experiment in your cooking, or even to visit France in search of the tarts I describe, then my work in compiling these recipes will have been even more rewarding.

Lastly, I should like to extend my thanks to my dear friends who contributed to this lighthearted collection. Their sense of humour is such that they are willing to be linked with all the innuendos associated with tarts, especially of the French variety.

Tips for Tarts

Tarts are simple to make but often appear daunting to
some cooks. This is usually due to concern over the pastry,
but armed with a foolproof recipe for basic pastry
(and variations) you can make any and all of the tarts which
are given in this book.

Foolproof Pastry

METRIC/IMPERIAL	AMERICAN
500g/1lb plain flour	4 cups all-purpose flour
175g/6oz butter	¾ cup butter
125g/4oz lard	½ cup shortening
2 tablespoons caster sugar (optional)	2 tablespoons superfine sugar (optional)
1 egg and 1 yolk, beaten	1 egg and 1 yolk, beaten
1½ tablespoons cold water	1½ tablespoons cold water

1. Sift the flour into a bowl, and cut the fat into the flour with a knife. Rub the fat into the flour with your fingertips until the mixture resembles breadcrumbs. (Here you may add 2 table-spoons caster sugar if you want sweet pastry).
2. Mix in the beaten eggs followed by the water.
3. Wrap the dough in greaseproof paper or plastic film and leave in the refrigerator to rest for about twenty minutes before using. This quantity will make two tarts.

Pastry Problems

Most French cooks are adamant that pastry cannot do justice to their cooking if it is made using margarine, and lard is not available in France. Soft margarine is even less successful. Of course, if you are making pastry for a savoury tart, a quarter of the fat may be replaced by lard.

Many people are poor pastry cooks – their hands are too warm or their action is too heavy. I recommend the use of a food processor for these unfortunate people. Undoubtedly, the secret for perfect pastry is to have all ingredients and equip-ment ice cold. And remember, add just enough ice cold water to mix, not to make it sticky. Add it little by little, then the perfect texture will be reached. Always chill the pastry for about 20 minutes or more before using. This makes it easier to handle, reduces shrinkage and should result in perfect pastry every time.

When rolling the pastry out, keep the surface and rolling pin lightly floured to prevent sticking. Don't handle the pastry too much as this will make the result much heavier. Roll lightly, away from you and turn the pastry after each roll, but never turn the pastry over.

Professional cooks recommend that tarts should be baked in a loose-bottomed metal flan tin, but I find these loose-based tins are a hindrance rather than a help. Porcelain or earthen-ware flan dishes look very attractive on the table and, what's more, will hold any mixture with a tendency to run.

Baking Blind

Baking blind is often a subject of contention. Flan cases are generally pre-baked without the filling to give a crisp pastry shell that holds its shape, and to prevent a soggy base from forming. It is usual to bake the raw pastry 'blind'. The uncooked pastry case is lined with greaseproof paper or foil and half-filled with rice or dried beans. The case is then baked until barely done, then the paper and filling is removed and the case returned to the oven for a few minutes to dry out.

After many attempts at the process, I've concluded that washed gravel is to be recommended. Line the flan case with greaseproof paper and cover with a layer of gravel. If the stones are evenly positioned they will prevent the edge from collap-sing inwards and the base from 'bubbling'.

However, I find if I prick the case thoroughly with a fork, and then freeze it for about 20 minutes immediately before baking, the pastry case is cooked quickly and effectively with no covering whatsoever.

Good Companions

With the right escort a tart comes into its own. Who can tell which is the 'better half'? I shall play safe and claim that savoury tarts served with salads (dressed of course), and sweet tarts served with a sorbet or sauce make a marvellous team.

The French tend to like their food nature, plain without sauce or accompaniment of any kind. Nevertheless they do lead the field in the art of making the vinaigrettes and mayonnaises which give bite to their salads and garnishes. Both dressings are usually oil based, but I have been careful to include some less fattening alternatives towards the end of this collection of recipes. However calorie conscious you may be though, you should never leave a salad undressed. If you are dieting simply toss your salad in lemon juice and a mixture of fresh herbs and your virtue will remain intact.

The presentation of a salad is all important, and fresh herbs add a magical touch. My thanks must go to Christine, who taught me the delights of the herb garden and inspired me to add borage flowers, chickweed and rose petals to my salads.

A savoury tart can also be enhanced by an unusual arrangement of crudités, tossed in a vinaigrette and served with crusty French bread.

It is sheer indulgence and therefore wonderful to offer a cream sauce or ice cream with a sweet tart. Similarly, chopped fresh fruits may be mixed with whipped cream to create a topping with a difference.

Naughty...
but nice

Despite their crusty exteriors, all these tarts are renowned
for their sweet and sumptuous nature, and the mouth-
watering combinations of fruits, cream and meringue are
irresistible to most people. Tarts are always acceptable
when entertaining and even the family will appreciate
their delicious, rich character and tasty appeal.

Fabienne

Fabienne and Norman live in an exquisite house surrounded by orchards and soft-fruit farms. The friendly farmers offer her their fruits in return for the tarts she can provide.

Tarte aux Pêches Amandine
(Almond and Peach Tart)

METRIC/IMPERIAL
Pastry:
200g/7oz plain flour
100g/3½oz butter
75g/3oz sugar
1 egg yolk
2 tablespoons cold water
Filling:
75g/3oz butter
40g/1½oz caster sugar
2 egg yolks
65g/2½oz ground almonds
1 tablespoon cornflour
salt
1 × 410g/14½oz can peach halves

AMERICAN
Pastry:
1¾ cups all-purpose flour
½ cup butter
6 tablespoons sugar
1 egg yolk
2 tablespoons cold water
Filling:
6 tablespoons butter
3 tablespoons sugar
2 egg yolks
generous ½ cup ground almonds
1 tablespoon cornstarch
salt
1 × 15oz can peach halves

1. To make the pastry, sift the flour into a bowl. Dice the butter into the flour and rub in (cut in). Stir in the sugar followed by the egg yolk. Mix to a dough with the cold water and leave to rest in the refrigerator for 30 minutes. Roll the dough out onto a floured surface and use it to line a buttered, deep 22cm/8½ inch flan dish or tart pan.
2. To make the filling, cream the butter, add the sugar and egg yolks and beat well with a wooden spoon. Stir in the ground almonds, the cornflour (cornstarch) and a pinch of salt.
3. Prick the pastry with a fork. Spread the filling over the base of the tart and arrange the peach halves on top, cut side down. Press the fruit down with your fingertips.
4. Bake in a preheated moderately hot oven (190°C/375°F, Gas Mark 5) for 30 minutes. Serve warm or cold. If you are not intending to eat this tart immediately do not place it in the refrigerator – the pastry will go soft. Place it in an airtight tin and store in a cool place.

Tarte aux Poires
(Pear Tart)

METRIC/IMPERIAL
Pastry:
200g/7oz plain flour
salt
100g/3½oz butter
3 tablespoons cold milk
Filling:
250ml/8 fl oz double cream
2 egg yolks
2 tablespoons caster sugar
1 tablespoon Calvados or sherry
4 large pears, peeled

AMERICAN
Pastry:
1¾ cups all-purpose flour
salt
½ cup butter
3 tablespoons cold milk
Filling:
1 cup heavy cream
2 egg yolks
2 tablespoons sugar
1 tablespoon applejack or sherry
4 large pears, peeled

1. To make the pastry, sift the flour and a pinch of salt into a bowl. Dice the butter into the flour and rub in (cut in), then mix to a dough with the milk. Leave to rest in the refrigerator for 20 minutes, then roll it out on a floured surface and use it to line a buttered, deep 22cm/8½ inch flan dish or tart pan. Prick the base lightly with a fork and bake blind in a preheated moderately hot oven (200°C/400°F, Gas Mark 6) for about 10 minutes, until the pastry has begun to form a slight crust.
2. For the filling, beat together the cream, egg yolks, sugar and Calvados (applejack) or sherry.
3. Halve the pears and remove the core with a teaspoon. Make vertical slices in the pear halves without cutting all the way through (see photograph opposite). Place them, flat sides down, in the pastry case. Cover the pears with the filling and return to the oven for 30 minutes.

Tarte aux Poires (left) and Tarte aux Pêches Amandine (right) ▷

Marie-Thérèse

When she was a little girl, Marie-Thérèse loved Nanny brushing her hair 100 times a night. Now she's a big girl, her hairbrush is still very much part of her bed-time routine.

Tarte à l'Orange
(Orange Tart)

METRIC/IMPERIAL
Pastry:
200g/7oz plain flour
100g/3½oz butter
3 tablespoons cold water
Filling:
300ml/½ pint milk
grated rind and juice of 3
  oranges
2 whole eggs
3 egg yolks
125g/4oz caster sugar
40g/1½oz plain flour,
  sifted
To decorate:
1 orange, sliced
whipped cream

AMERICAN
Pastry:
1¾ cups all-purpose flour
½ cup butter
3 tablespoons cold water
Filling:
1¼ cups milk
grated rind and juice of 3
  oranges
2 whole eggs
3 egg yolks
½ cup sugar
6 tablespoons all-purpose flour,
  sifted
To decorate:
1 orange, sliced
whipped cream

1. To make the pastry, sift the flour into a bowl. Dice the butter into the flour and rub in (cut in), then mix to a dough with the cold water. Roll out the dough on a floured surface and use it to line a buttered 22cm/8½ inch round flan dish or tart pan. Place a few extra knobs of butter on the pastry and leave in the refrigerator.
2. To make the filling, first boil the milk; add the grated orange rind to it.
3. In a bowl beat together the eggs and egg yolks with the sugar. Beat until pale. Stir in the sifted flour a little at a time. Add the juice of the oranges; finally stir in the warm milk. Leave until cold.
4. Pour the cold orange filling into the cold unbaked pastry case. Bake in a preheated moderately hot oven (190°C/375°F, Gas Mark 5) for 40 minutes. Serve warm, decorated with slices of fresh orange and piped cream.

◁ *Tarte à l'Orange*

Flan aux Mûres
(Blackberry Flan)

METRIC/IMPERIAL
400g/14oz blackberries, washed
150g/5oz sugar
125g/4oz plain flour
3 eggs
250ml/8fl oz milk
1 tablespoon double cream

AMERICAN
1½ cups blackberries, washed
⅔ cup sugar, firmly packed
1 cup all-purpose flour
3 eggs
1 cup milk
1 tablespoon heavy cream

1. Mix the blackberries with the sugar and leave to stand for about an hour.
2. Using a wooden spoon, beat the flour with the eggs. Stir in the milk a little at a time. Add the cream.
3. Mix the egg and milk mixture with the fruit and pour into a buttered 22cm/8½ inch flan dish or tart pan. The mixture should come two-thirds of the way up the sides of the dish.
4. Bake in a preheated moderate oven (180°C/350°F, Gas Mark 4) for 30 to 40 minutes.
5. Serve this tart warm with vanilla ice cream (see page 82); or cold with cream.

Joëlle

*Love-lorn soldiers once posted heart-shaped cheeses to their
loved ones back home. Alas, their hearts were often sadly battered.
Joëlle ensures that her tarts' hearts are never even bruised.*

Tarte aux Framboises
(Raspberry Tart)

METRIC/IMPERIAL	AMERICAN
Pastry:	**Pastry:**
200g/7oz plain flour	1¾ cups all-purpose flour
salt	salt
100g/3½oz butter	½ cup butter
1 tablespoon caster sugar	1 tablespoon sugar
1 egg, beaten	1 egg, beaten
2 tablespoons cold water	2 tablespoons cold water
Filling:	**Filling:**
250g/8oz cream cheese	1 cup cream cheese
1 tablespoon sugar	1 tablespoon sugar
500g/1lb fresh raspberries, washed	1lb fresh raspberries, washed
Glaze:	**Glaze:**
3 tablespoons redcurrant jelly	3 tablespoons redcurrant jelly
1 tablespoon Cointreau	1 tablespoon Cointreau

1. To make the pastry, sift the flour and a pinch of salt into a bowl. Dice the butter into the flour and rub in (cut in). Stir in the sugar and bind with the egg. Mix to a dough with the cold water. Leave the dough to rest in a cool place for 20 minutes before rolling it out on a floured surface. Line a buttered 22cm/8½ inch flan dish or tart pan. Prick the base lightly with a fork and bake blind in a preheated moderately hot oven (200°C/400°F, Gas Mark 6) for about 15 minutes, until the pastry has begun to form a crust. Remove the foil and continue to bake the pastry for a further 5 to 10 minutes until it is completely cooked. Leave to cool completely.
2. For the filling, beat together the cream cheese and sugar, spread over the pastry case, and cover with the raspberries.
3. Melt the redcurrant jelly in a small pan and boil until smooth, stirring all the time. Add the Cointreau. Brush the fruit with the glaze and serve cold. Eat within 24 hours.

Gâteau à l'Ananas
(Pineapple Cake)

METRIC/IMPERIAL	AMERICAN
4 eggs	4 eggs
200g/7oz sugar	1 cup sugar
160g/5oz butter	just under ¾ cup butter
160g/5oz self-raising flour	1¼ cups self-rising flour
½ teaspoon baking powder	½ teaspoon baking powder
1 × 227g/8oz can pineapple rings	1 × 8¼oz can pineapple rings
Caramel:	**Caramel:**
15g/½oz butter	1 tablespoon butter
1 tablespoon sugar	1 tablespoon sugar
rum	rum

1. Place the butter and sugar for the caramel in the base of a 22cm/8½ inch baking tin. Stir the sugar and butter together over a protective plate over a medium heat until a caramel has formed. Cool completely.
2. Using a wooden spoon beat together the eggs and the sugar. Beat in the butter, flour and baking powder to give a cake-like mixture.
3. Place the rings of drained fruit over the caramel. Cover with the cake mixture.
4. Bake in a preheated moderately hot oven (190°C/375°F, Gas Mark 5) for 30 to 40 minutes until the cake is golden brown.
5. Make a few holes in the cake with a skewer. Mix some pineapple juice with rum to taste and pour over the cake, still in its tin. Cool completely and unmould so that the caramel is on the top. Serve with thickly whipped cream.

Tarte aux Framboises ▷

Kiki

*Kiki's parties never flop. She knows that saucy tarts, dressed
to kill, really make parties go off with a bang.*

Tartelettes au Citron
(Lemon Tartlets)

METRIC/IMPERIAL	AMERICAN
Pastry:	**Pastry:**
200g/7oz plain flour	1¾ cups all-purpose flour
salt	salt
100g/3½oz butter	½ cup butter
1 egg yolk	1 egg yolk
2 tablespoons cold water	2 tablespoons cold water
Filling:	**Filling:**
1 egg	1 egg
150g/5oz sugar	⅔ cup sugar
grated rind and juice of 1 lemon	grated rind and juice of 1 lemon
65g/2½oz butter	⅓ cup butter
crystallized lemon slices, to decorate	candied lemon slices, to decorate

1. To make the pastry, sift the flour and a pinch of salt into a bowl. Dice the butter into the flour and rub in (cut in). Stir in the egg yolk and mix to a dough with the water. leave the dough to rest in the refrigerator for 20 minutes before rolling out on a floured surface. Line 8 to 10 tartlet tins with the dough and prick the bases lightly with a fork.
2. For the filling, beat the egg with the sugar. Slowly stir in the lemon rind and juice. Soften the butter in the oven and incorporate with the lemon mixture. Pour this mixture into the tartlet cases.
3. Bake in a moderate oven (180°C/350°F, Gas Mark 4) for 25 minutes, until the filling has set and the pastry is fully cooked.
4. Cool the tarts completely and decorate with the crystallized (candied) lemon slices.

◁ *Tartelettes au Citron (left) and Bande de Fruits (right)*

Bande de Fruits
(Fruit Strip)

METRIC/IMPERIAL	AMERICAN
200g/7oz frozen puff pastry	7oz frozen puff pastry
Pastry cream:	**Pastry cream:**
2 egg yolks, beaten	2 egg yolks, beaten
150ml/¼ pint milk	⅔ cup milk
1 tablespoon cornflour	1 tablespoon cornstarch
2 tablespoons sugar	2 tablespoons sugar
vanilla essence	vanilla
Fruit filling:	**Fruit filling:**
125g/4oz maraschino cherries	1 cup maraschino cherries
1 mango, peeled and sliced	1 mango, peeled and sliced
2 rings pineapple, diced	2 rings pineapple, diced
1 kiwifruit, sliced	1 kiwifruit, sliced
125g/4oz raspberries	⅔ cup raspberries
Glaze:	**Glaze:**
2 tablespoons apricot jam	2 tablespoons apricot jam
1 tablespoon water	1 tablespoon water

1. Defrost and roll the pastry into a rectangle about 12cm/5 inches wide. Fold in half lengthwise. Cut a 1cm/½ inch band from around the three open edges. Open out the rectangle and roll again so that it is 2cm/1 inch wider and longer. Place on a dampened baking sheet, prick with a fork and dampen the edges. Open the band of pastry and press on to the rectangle to make a border. Prick the base with a fork and bake for 10 minutes in a preheated moderately hot oven (200°C/400°F, Gas Mark 6). Reduce oven temperature to 160°C/325°F, Gas Mark 3, and cook for a further 15 minutes; cool.
2. To make the pastry cream, boil the milk in a small pan. In a bowl mix together the cornflour (cornstarch), sugar and egg yolks. Pour the milk onto the egg mixture together with a few drops of vanilla essence. Return to the pan and cook slowly over a low heat stirring all the time with a wooden spoon until it has thickened. Cool.
3. Spread the pastry cream onto the cooked pastry case. Arrange the fruits on the pastry cream.
4. For the glaze: boil the apricot jam in a small pan with the water until it is smooth. Brush lightly over the fruits.

17

Céline

Céline is an active lady whose outdoor pursuits give her an almost insatiable appetite. But when the weather is unkind, she is equally happy to participate in indoor games.

Tarte au Riz
(Rice Tart)

METRIC/IMPERIAL	AMERICAN
Pastry:	**Pastry:**
250g/8oz plain flour	2 cups all-purpose flour
salt	salt
125g/4oz butter	½ cup butter
125g/4oz sugar	½ cup sugar
1 egg, beaten	1 egg, beaten
Filling:	**Filling:**
400ml/14fl oz milk	1¾ cups milk
vanilla essence	vanilla
100g/3½oz pudding rice	7 tablespoons pudding rice
75g/3oz sugar	6 tablespoons sugar
2 tablespoons cream	2 tablespoons cream
1egg, beaten	1 egg, beaten
50g/2oz crystallized ginger	¼ cup candied ginger
50g/2oz crystallized pineapple	¼ cup candied pineapple
2 tablespoons rum	2 tablespoons rum
2 egg whites, whisked	2 egg whites, whisked
40g/1½oz butter	3 tablespoons butter
5 sugar lumps	5 sugar cubes

1. To make the pastry, sift the flour and a pinch of salt into a bowl. Dice the butter into the flour and rub in (cut in). Stir in the sugar and then the beaten egg; mix to a dough with the cold water. Chill for at least 1 hour. Roll it out onto a floured surface and line a buttered 25cm/10 inch flan dish or tart pan.
2. To make the filling, boil the milk with a few drops of vanilla essence. Wash the rice and add it to the milk. Half cover the pan and leave to simmer for 25 minutes.
3. Remove from the heat and stir in a pinch of salt, the sugar, cream, egg, fruit and rum. Fold in the egg whites.
4. Place this mixture into the unbaked pastry case. Melt the butter in a small pan and pour over followed by the sugar cubes, crumbling them slightly as you do so.
5. Bake in a preheated moderately hot oven (190°C/375°F, Gas Mark 5) for 30 to 35 minutes. Serve hot.

Enveloppe aux Abricots
(Apricot Envelope)

METRIC/IMPERIAL	AMERICAN
500g/1 lb frozen puff pastry	1 lb frozen puff pastry
Almond paste:	**Almond paste:**
75g/3 oz butter	⅓ cup butter
75g/3 oz caster sugar	⅓ cup sugar
1 tablespoon plain flour	1 tablespoon all-purpose flour
75g/3 oz ground almonds	⅔ cup ground almonds
almond essence	almond extract
1½ eggs	1½ eggs
Filling:	**Filling:**
1 × 411g/14½ oz can apricots	1 × 16 oz can apricots
½ egg	½ egg
1 teaspoon sugar	1 teaspoon sugar
1 tablespoon icing sugar, to decorate	1 tablespoon confectioners' sugar, to decorate

1. Roll out the defrosted pastry into a square.
2. To make the almond paste, cream together the butter and caster sugar. Add the flour and stir in well. Add the ground almonds and a few drops of almond essence and mix to a cream with the eggs.
3. Spread the almond paste on the square of pastry. Using a blender or a food processor, purée the drained apricots and spread them over the paste. Pull up the four corners of the pastry to make an envelope. Brush the remaining ½ egg and teaspoon of sugar over each of the four triangles of pastry.
4. Bake the tart in a preheated hot oven (220°C/425°F, Gas Mark 7) for 10 minutes. Reduce the heat to 200°C/400°F, Gas Mark 6 for a further 15 to 20 minutes. Just before the tart is cooked sprinkle it with the icing (confectioners') sugar. Serve warm or cold.

Tarte au Riz (left) and Enveloppe aux Abricots (right); Tartelettes aux Raisins (above), for recipe see page 21 ▷

Martine

Martine is a very busy and efficient secretary. Her culinary skills are matched only by those she uses in the office when attending to the needs of her boss.

Tartelettes aux Raisins
(Grape Tartlets)

METRIC/IMPERIAL
Pastry:
200g/7oz plain flour
salt
100g/3½oz butter
3 tablespoons cold water
Filling:
300g/10oz white grapes, pips
    removed
125g/4oz black grapes, pips
    removed
2 eggs
3 tablespoons sugar
3 tablespoons ground almonds
6 tablespoons double cream

AMERICAN
Pastry:
1¾ cups all-purpose flour
salt
½ cup butter
3 tablespoons cold water
Filling:
2½ cups green grapes, seeds
    removed
1 cup purple grapes, seeds
    removed
2 eggs
3 tablespoons sugar
3 tablespoons ground almonds
6 tablespoons heavy cream

1. Sift the flour and a pinch of salt into a bowl. Dice the butter into the flour and rub in (cut in), then mix to a dough with the cold water. Roll out the dough on a floured surface and line individual tartlet tins. Bake blind in a preheated moderately hot oven (200°C/400°F, Gas Mark 6) for 5 minutes.
2. For the filling, arrange the grapes in the pastry cases.
3. Beat together the eggs with the sugar, then add the ground almonds and stir in the cream. Spoon this mixture onto the grapes, smoothing the surface. Reduce the oven temperature to 190°C/375°F, Gas Mark 5, and bake the tarts for 15 minutes. Serve cold.

◁ *Tartelettes aux Abricots*

Tartelettes aux Abricots
(Apricot tartlets)

METRIC/IMPERIAL
Pastry:
200g/7oz plain flour
salt
100g/3½oz butter
3 tablespoons cold water
Pastry cream:
2 egg yolks
2 tablespoons sugar
1 tablespoon cornflour
150ml/¼ pint milk
3 tablespoons apricot jam
1 × 411g/14½oz can apricot
    halves
1 tablespoon water
tiny mint leaves, to decorate

AMERICAN
Pastry:
1¾ cups all-purpose flour
salt
½ cup butter
3 tablespoons cold water
Pastry cream:
2 egg yolks
2 tablespoons sugar
1 tablespoon cornstarch
⅔ cup milk
3 tablespoons apricot jam
1 × 16oz can apricot halves
1 tablespoon water
tiny mint leaves, to decorate

1. Sift the flour and a pinch of salt into a bowl. Dice the butter into the flour and run in (cut in), then mix to a dough with the water. Roll out the dough on a floured surface and line buttered individual tartlet tins. Prick the bases lightly with a fork and bake blind in a preheated moderately hot oven (200°C/400°F, Gas Mark 6) for about 10 minutes, until the pastry has begun to form a slight crust.
2. Martine always cheated when making pastry cream and it never failed. Using a fork, mix together the egg yolks, sugar and cornflour (cornstarch) in a small pan. Slowly whisk in a little of the milk. Place the pan over a low heat and continue to whisk while you add the rest of the milk. Stir until it is smooth and thick. Remove the pan from the heat. Spread 1 tablespoon of the apricot jam over the base of the pastry case followed by the pastry cream.
3. Drain the apricots and arrange them in the tartlets. Decorate with the mint leaves.
4. Melt the remaining jam in a pan with the water and boil until smooth. Pour or brush over the fruit.
5. Return the tarts to the oven for a further 5 to 10 minutes.

Christine

This pre-Raphaelite beauty spent a year in Paris cooking beefburgers for children. Her fortunes changed when she met a romantic Englishman who strews roses in her path and postpones tea for one in favour of games for two.

Tarte à la Figue
(Fig Tart)

Pastry:
200g/7oz plain flour
salt
100g/3½oz butter
3 tablespoons cold water
Filling:
150ml/¼ pint milk
2 egg yolks
2 tablespoons caster sugar
1 tablespoon cornflour
250g/8oz dried figs, sliced
2 tablespoons apricot jam
1 tablespoon water

Pastry:
1¾ cups all-purpose flour
salt
½ cup butter
3 tablespoons cold water
Filling:
⅔ cup milk
2 egg yolks
2 tablespoons sugar
1 tablespoon cornstarch
½lb dried figs, sliced
2 tablespoons apricot jam
1 tablespoon water

1. To make the pastry, sift the flour and a pinch of salt into a bowl. Dice the butter into the flour and rub in (cut in), then mix to a dough with the cold water. Roll out the dough on a floured surface and line a buttered 22cm/8½ inch flan dish or tart pan. Bake blind in a preheated moderately hot oven (200°C/400°F, Gas Mark 6) for 15 minutes, until the pastry has formed a slight crust.
2. To make the filling, boil the milk in a small pan. Meanwhile whisk together the egg yolks, sugar and cornflour (cornstarch) in a medium bowl. Pour the milk onto the mixture and stir well. Return to the heat and cook slowly until it thickens, stirring all the time with a wooden spoon. Cool.
3. Spread this pastry cream over the pastry case. Arrange the sliced figs over the pastry cream, letting the cream show through.
4. Boil the apricot jam with the water in a small pan until smooth and thick. Brush this lightly over the figs and return to the oven for a further 10 minutes. Serve cold.

Tarte au Miel et aux Noix
(Honey and Nut Tart)

METRIC/IMPERIAL
Pastry:
200g/7oz plain flour
salt
100g/3½oz butter
1 teaspoon sugar
3 tablespoons cold water
Filling:
250g/8oz shelled walnuts
500g/1lb clear honey

AMERICAN
Pastry:
1¾ cups all-purpose flour
salt
½ cup butter
1 teaspoon sugar
3 tablespoons cold water
Filling:
2 cups shelled walnuts
1lb honey

1. To make the pastry, sift the flour and a pinch of salt into a bowl. Dice the butter into the flour and rub in (cut in). Stir in the sugar and mix to a dough with the cold water. Roll out on to a floured surface and line a 22cm/8½ inch flan dish or tart pan. Prick the case lightly with a fork and bake blind in a moderately hot oven (200°C/400°F, Gas Mark 6) for 20 minutes until almost cooked.
2. Reserve 8 walnut halves for decoration. For the filling, roughly chop the remainder and mix them with the honey. Pour this into the pastry case and return to the oven for 10 minutes.
3. Decorate the tart with the reserved walnut halves. Serve warm or cold.

Tarte au Miel et aux Noix ▷

Paule

*A flute and a cello harmonize well with each other and Paule and
her partner often play together in perfect accord.*

Coeur de Poires au Chocolat

(Chocolate Pear Heart)

METRIC/IMPERIAL	AMERICAN
2 large pears, peeled and sliced	2 large pears, peeled and sliced
100g/3½oz self-raising flour	1 cup self-rising flour
100g/3½oz butter	½ cup butter
2 eggs	2 eggs
100g/3½oz caster sugar	½ cup sugar
1½ tablespoons cocoa powder	1½ tablespoons unsweetened cocoa
1 teaspoon instant coffee granules dissolved in 1 tablespoon hot water	1 teaspoon instant coffee granules dissolved in 1 tablespoon hot water
½ teaspoon baking powder	½ teaspoon baking powder
1 tablespoon Calvados	1 tablespoon applejack

1. Line a heart-shaped baking tin with greaseproof (waxed) paper. Arrange the pear slices on the greaseproof (waxed) paper in the baking tin.
2. Using an electric mixer or food processor mix together the flour, butter, eggs, sugar, cocoa, liquid coffee, baking powder until smooth.
3. Spread this mixture over the pears and level the surface.
4. Bake in a moderately hot oven (190°C/375°F, Gas Mark 5) for 30 to 35 minutes until it has the appearance of a fully baked cake. Unmould the cake and leave it to cool on a wire rack with the pears uppermost. Serve cold, sprinkled with the Calvados (applejack) and accompanied by cream or ice cream.

Galette de Perouges

(Perouges Girdle Cake)

METRIC/IMPERIAL	AMERICAN
2 teaspoons active dried yeast	2 teaspoons dried yeast
2 tablespoons sugar	2 tablespoons sugar
2 tablespoons hot water	2 tablespoons hot water
200g/7oz flour	1¾ cups all-purpose flour
salt	salt
1 egg, beaten	1 egg, beaten
grated rind of 1 lemon	grated rind of 1 lemon
150g/5oz butter, softened	just under ¾ cup softened butter
icing sugar to decorate	confectioners' sugar to decorate

1. Dissolve the yeast and ½ teaspoon of the sugar in the hot water. Leave to stand, stirring occasionally, until the yeast is frothy.
2. Sift the flour and salt into a bowl and add the yeast, egg and lemon rind. Beat together, gradually adding the softened butter. Knead the dough thoroughly until it comes cleanly away from the sides of the bowl.
3. Cover the bowl with a damp cloth and leave the dough to prove in a warm place for 1½ to 2 hours or until doubled in size.
4. Using the palms of your hands, press the dough out into a 25cm/10 inch circle. Place on a greased and floured baking sheet and fold over a 15mm/1 inch lip all the way round the edge. Sprinkle with sifted icing (confectioners') sugar.
5. Bake in a preheated very hot oven (240°C/475°F, Gas Mark 9) for 8 to 10 minutes until the edges of the Galette are golden. Cool on a wire rack.

◁ *Coeur de Poires au Chocolat*

Marie-Pierre

*"Uneasy lies the head that wears a crown," and actress Marie-Pierre
finds that she is no exception. Nicknamed "the Queen of Hearts"
she finds her crown gets in the way at bedtime and happily removes
it along with everything else.*

Galette des Rois à la Frangipane

(Twelfth-Night Frangipane Cake)

This tart is eaten in France to celebrate Twelfth Night. It is
available in all the pâtisseries and comes complete with gold
and silver cardboard crowns. Inside the cake two *fèves* or china
beans have been planted; one will represent the king and the
other his Queen. Whichever lucky couple should find the *fèves*
must don their crowns and may bask in temporary glory and
the privileges of sovereignty.

METRIC/IMPERIAL	AMERICAN
100g/3½oz ground almonds	*scant 1 cup ground almonds*
100g/3½oz icing sugar, sifted	*¾ cup confectioners' sugar, sifted*
1 whole egg and 1 yolk	*1 whole egg and 1 yolk*
50g/2oz butter, softened	*¼ cup butter, softened*
2 tablespoons Cointreau	*2 tablespoons Cointreau*
400g/14oz frozen puff pastry	*14oz frozen puff pastry*
2 china beans or silver coins	*2 china beans or silver coins*

1. Make the frangipane by beating together the ground
almonds, sugar, the whole egg, softened butter and the
Cointreau.
2. Roll the fully defrosted pastry out on a floured surface into
the shape of a rectangle. Cut two circles out of this using a
22cm/8½ inch flan dish or tart pan as a template. Make one
circle the size of the dish, the other 2.5cm/1 inch larger.
3. Butter the same flan dish or tart pan and line it with the
larger circle of pastry. Spread the frangipane over the pastry.
Hide the *fèves* in the mixture. Wet the edges of the pastry with
a little water and place the remaining circle on top. Seal the
pastry by pressing the edges together. Beat the remaining egg
yolk with a little water and brush the surface of the galette.
4. Using the back of a knife make a lattice pattern on the top
and bake in a preheated hot oven (220°C/425°F, Gas Mark 7)
for 20 minutes. The cake may be served hot or cold.

Clafouti aux Cerises

(Cherry Clafouti)

METRIC/IMPERIAL	AMERICAN
75g/3oz plain flour	*¾ cup all-purpose flour*
125g/4oz sugar	*½ cup sugar*
250ml/8fl oz milk	*1 cup milk*
6 eggs, beaten	*6 eggs, beaten*
750g/1½lb stoned black cherries, halved	*4½ cups pitted bing cherries, halved*
kirsch	*kirsch*

1. In a large bowl mix together the flour, 100g/3½oz (7
tablespoons) sugar and the eggs, using a wooden spoon. Add a
little of the milk and beat until smooth.
2. Slowly stir in the rest of the milk until the consistency is
similar to that of pancake batter. Stir in the halved cherries
and a splash of kirsch.
3. Butter a large ovenproof dish. (I like to use an oval 'au
gratin' dish.) Pour in the mixture.
4. Bake in a preheated moderately hot oven (190°C/375°F,
Gas Mark 5) for 35 minutes. Serve cold, sprinkled with the
remaining sugar.

Galette des Rois à la Frangipane ▷

27

Annie

*This Breton lady frequents all the summer folk festivals as she loves
dancing the traditional reels to the strains of bagpipe music.
When the dancing is over, her partners often persuade her to join
them in other invigorating pursuits.*

Far Breton

This traditional Breton dish is extremely filling and quite
delicious. The people of Brittany favour the use of prunes in
their cooking and are responsible for the success of this dish.

METRIC/IMPERIAL	AMERICAN
6 eggs	6 eggs
200g/7oz caster sugar	1 cup sugar
200g/7oz plain flour	1¾ cups all-purpose flour
salt	salt
1 litre/1¾ pints milk	4¼ cups milk
200g/7oz halved prunes	1¼ cups halved prunes

1. Beat together the eggs with the sugar. Slowly and gradually
stir in the flour until it is smooth; add a large pinch of salt. Stir
in the milk a little at a time until the consistency is smooth
and rather like a thick batter.
2. Butter a very large, deep ovenproof dish about 25cm/10
inch square. Stir the halved prunes into the milk mixture and
pour into the dish.
3. Bake the Far in a preheated moderately hot oven (180°C/
350°F, Gas Mark 4) for 1¼ to 1½ hours until it has set and is
golden brown.

Gâteau Breton

The Bretons often slice this cake in half and spread the inside
with puréed poached prunes.

METRIC/IMPERIAL	AMERICAN
5 egg yolks	5 egg yolks
250g/8oz caster sugar	1 cup sugar
250g/8oz butter, softened	1 cup butter, softened
350g/11oz plain flour	2¾ cups all-purpose flour
½ teaspoon baking powder	½ teaspoon baking powder
To decorate:	**To decorate:**
1 egg yolk	1 egg yolk
1 tablespoon milk	1 tablespoon milk

1. Mix together the egg yolks, sugar and the softened butter.
Slowly stir in the flour a little at a time together with the
baking powder.
2. Butter a 18cm/7 inch round baking tin (pan), spoon the
cake mixture into the tin and smooth over the surface, making
sure that it is level. Brush the surface with the remaining yolk
and milk.
3. Bake in a preheated moderately hot oven (190°C/375°F,
Gas Mark 5) for 40 minutes until the surface is golden brown.
4. Unmould the cooked cake and invert it onto a baking rack
in order to create a criss-cross design. Serve the Gâteau Breton
when completely cool.

◁ *Gâteau Breton (left) and Far Breton (right)*

Veronique

A lover of keep-fit and all forms of physical exercise, she left her overweight husband, who enjoyed tarts too much, and pedalled away with the man who owns the bicycle shop.

Flan aux Poires
(Pear Cake)

This is an exceptionally simple dessert to make but the generous splash of alcohol added lifts it right out of the ordinary. The flan may be made with apples instead of pears and served hot or cold although I think it is most delicious eaten hot with vanilla ice cream. It can be baked in a shallow mould of any shape – I like to use a 30 × 20cm/12 × 8 inch ovenproof dish.

METRIC/IMPERIAL	AMERICAN
200g/7oz butter	1 scant cup butter
200g/7oz caster sugar	1 cup sugar
3 eggs, beaten	3 eggs, beaten
200g/7oz self-raising flour	1¾ cups self-rising flour
salt	salt
½ teaspoon baking powder	½ teaspoon baking powder
2 tablespoons Calvados (or sherry)	2 tablespoons applejack (or sherry)
5 to 6 pears or apples, peeled, cored and chopped	5 to 6 pears or apples, peeled, cored and chopped

1. Cream together the butter and sugar until light and fluffy. Beat in the eggs.
2. Sift together the flour, a pinch of salt and baking powder. Fold into the mixture and mix well. Stir in the Calvados (applejack).
3. Fold the chopped pears or apples into the mixture and spread it into a buttered dish.
4. Bake in a preheated moderately hot oven (190°C/375°F, Gas Mark 5) for 30 minutes.

Tarte aux Prunes de Damas
(Damson Tart)

METRIC/IMPERIAL	AMERICAN
Pastry:	**Pastry:**
200g/7oz plain flour	1¾ cups all-purpose flour
100g/3½oz butter	½ cup butter
1 tablespoon sugar	1 tablespoon sugar
1 egg, beaten	1 egg, beaten
2 tablespoons cold water	2 tablespoons cold water
Filling:	**Filling:**
500g/1lb damsons or plums, halved and stoned	4 cups pitted damsons or plums, halved
2 tablespoons caster sugar	2 tablespoons sugar
2 tablespoons redcurrant jelly	2 tablespoons red currant jelly
1 tablespoon water	1 tablespoon water

1. To make the pastry, sift the flour into a bowl. Dice the butter into the flour and rub in (cut in). Stir in the sugar followed by the beaten egg, then mix to a dough with the cold water. Leave to rest in the refrigerator for 20 minutes before rolling out on a floured surface. Line a rectangular 35 × 10cm/ 14 × 4 inch tart pan with the dough and prick lightly with a fork.
2. For the filling, arrange the halved damsons, cut side down, over the pastry and sprinkle with the caster sugar.
3. Boil together the redcurrant jelly with the water until smooth and brush over the fruit.
4. Bake in a preheated moderately hot oven (200°C/400°F, Gas Mark 6) for 30 minutes and serve hot or cold. This recipe could well be adapted to make attractive little tartlets too.

Tarte aux Prunes de Damas ▷

Daphne

Tarts fit for a king, and Daphne always makes sure that all she provides is worth every penny.

Tartelettes aux Fraises

(Strawberry Tartlets)

METRIC/IMPERIAL
Pastry:
200g/7oz plain flour
salt
100g/3½oz butter
1 tablespoon sugar
1 egg yolk
2 tablespoons cold water
Filling:
3 tablespoons redcurrant jelly
200ml/⅓ pint double cream, whipped
500g/1lb strawberries, washed
2 tablespoons caster sugar
1 tablespoon water

AMERICAN
Pastry:
1¾ cups all-purpose flour
salt
½ cup butter
1 tablespoon sugar
1 egg yolk
2 tablespoons cold water
Filling:
3 tablespoons redcurrant jelly
⅞ cup heavy cream, whipped
1lb strawberries, washed
2 tablespoons sugar
1 tablespoon water

1. Sift the flour and a pinch of salt into a bowl. Dice the butter into the flour and rub in (cut in), then stir in the sugar and bind with the egg yolk. Mix to a dough with the cold water. Roll out the pastry on a floured surface and line 6 to 8 individual tartlet tins. Prick the bases lightly with a fork and bake blind in a preheated moderately hot oven (200°C/400°F, Gas Mark 6) for about 15 minutes, until the pastry is cooked. Remove the aluminium foil and return the pastry to the oven for another 5 minutes until the cases are golden.
2. Cool the cases completely and then brush each base with a little jam – reserve some of it for a glaze. Pipe swirls of cream on to each layer of jam and arrange the whole strawberries on top. Sprinkle with the sugar.
3. Melt the remaining jam with the water and boil until smooth. Brush over the strawberries. Eat within 24 hours. The taste of summer!

Tartelettes aux Reines Claudes

(Greengage Tartlets)

METRIC/IMPERIAL
Pastry:
200g/7oz plain flour
salt
100g/3½oz butter
3 tablespoons cold water
Filling:
500g/1lb greengages, halved and stoned
50g/2oz caster sugar
Glaze:
2 tablespoons apricot jam
1 tablespoon water

AMERICAN
Pastry:
1¾ cups all-purpose flour
salt
½ cup butter
3 tablespoons cold water
Filling:
1lb greengages, halved and pitted
4 tablespoons sugar
Glaze:
2 tablespoons apricot jam
1 tablespoon water

1. To make the pastry, sift the flour and a pinch of salt into a bowl. Dice the butter into the flour and rub in (cut in), then mix to a dough with the cold water. Roll out the dough on a floured surface and use it to line individual buttered tartlet tins. Prick the bases lightly with a fork.
2. For the filling, place overlapping greengage halves in the pastry cases, cut side down. Sprinkle with the sugar.
3. Bake in a preheated hot oven (220°C/425°F, Gas Mark 7) for 8 to 10 minutes – the sugar on top of the tart should caramelize.
4. To make the glaze, boil together the apricot jam and the water in a small pan until smooth. Pour or brush over the cooked fruit in the tart. Serve cold.

◁ *Tartelettes aux Fraises and Tartelettes aux Reines Claudes*

Gabrielle

Unlucky in cards, lucky in love proves to be true in
Gabrielle's case. Her favourite game is strip poker,
and it's one she never minds losing.

Tarte aux Quetsches

(Plum Tart)

METRIC/IMPERIAL
Pastry:
200g/7oz plain flour
salt
100g/3½oz butter
3 tablespoons cold water
Filling:
1kg/2lb yellow plums, halved,
  stones reserved
300g/10oz caster sugar
4 eggs
150g/5oz plain flour
150ml/¼ pint milk
2 tablespoons eau-de-vie de
  prune (plum brandy),
  brandy or Calvados
1 tablespoon icing sugar, sifted

AMERICAN
Pastry:
1¾ cups all-purpose flour
salt
½ cup butter
3 tablespoons cold water
Filling:
2lb yellow plums, halved, pits
  reserved
1¼ cups sugar
4 eggs
1¼ cups all-purpose flour
⅔ cup milk
2 tablespoons eau-de-vie de
  prune (plum brandy),
  brandy or applejack
1 tablespoon confectioners'
  sugar, sifted

1. To make the pastry, sift the flour and a pinch of salt into a bowl. Dice the butter into the flour and rub in (cut in), then mix to a dough with the cold water. Roll out the dough on a floured surface and use it to line a buttered 22cm/8½ inch flan dish or tart pan. Prick the base lightly with a fork and bake blind in a preheated moderately hot oven (200°C/400°F, Gas Mark 6) for about 10 minutes, until the pastry has begun to form a slight crust.
2. To make the filling, tie up the plum stones (pits) in muslin (cheesecloth) and pound the bag briefly with a rolling pin to crack the stones. Place the bag in a pan with the plums, 200g/7oz (generous ¾ cup) caster sugar and a little water and cook for 15 minutes. Drain the fruit and discard the bag of stones.
3. Beat the eggs, add the flour, milk and the remaining sugar. Add the liqueur.
4. Arrange the drained fruit in the pastry case. Pour over the topping and return the tart to the oven for 30 minutes. Serve cool and sprinkled with the icing (confectioners') sugar.

Tarte aux Myrtilles

(Myrtille Tart)

Myrte, used in this recipe, is the traditional Corsican liqueur, made from myrtille berries on the island. Although it has the appearance of water it is of similar potency to brandy and has a thick, sweet, syrupy taste.

METRIC/IMPERIAL
Pastry:
200g/7oz plain flour
salt
100g/3½oz butter
3 tablespoons cold water
Filling:
250g/8oz myrtilles, blueberries
  or blackcurrants
250g/8oz raspberries
125g/4oz sugar
150ml/¼ pint double cream
2 eggs, beaten
1 tablespoon Myrte (optional)

AMERICAN
Pastry:
1¾ cups all-purpose flour
salt
½ cup butter
3 tablespoons cold water
Filling:
½lb myrtilles, blueberries or
  blackcurrants
½lb raspberries
½ cup sugar
⅔ cup heavy cream
2 eggs, beaten
1 tablespoon Myrte (optional)

1. Sift the flour and a pinch of salt into a bowl. Dice the butter into the flour and rub in (cut in), then mix to a dough with the water. Roll out the dough on a floured surface and line a buttered 22cm/8½ inch flan dish or tart pan. Prick the base lightly with a fork.
2. For the filling, mix together most of the sugar, the cream, beaten eggs and liqueur, if using; pour this into the unbaked pastry case and bake in a preheated moderately hot oven (190°C/375°F, Gas Mark 5) for 25 minutes.
3. Arrange the freshly prepared fruit on top and sprinkle with the remaining sugar. Return to the oven for a further 10 minutes. Serve hot or cold.

Tarte aux Myrtilles ▷

34

Micheline

As an art student, Micheline finds it helps inspire her creative muse to study not only old masters but younger ones, too.

Tarte à la Rhubarbe
(Rhubarb Tart)

METRIC/IMPERIAL	AMERICAN
Pastry:	**Pastry:**
200g/7oz plain flour	1¾ cups all-purpose flour
salt	salt
100g/3½oz butter	½ cup butter
3 tablespoons cold water	3 tablespoons cold water
Filling:	**Filling:**
500g/1lb rhubarb, thickly sliced	1lb rhubarb, thickly sliced
175g/6oz sugar	¾ cup sugar
2 eggs	2 eggs
50g/2oz plain flour	½ cup all-purpose flour
grated rind of 1 orange	grated rind of 1 orange
150ml/¼ pint double cream	⅔ cup heavy cream
Glaze:	**Glaze:**
2 tablespoons redcurrant jelly	2 tablespoons redcurrant jelly
1 tablespoon water	1 tablespoon water

1. The day before you want to make the tart, sprinkle the rhubarb with half the sugar and leave to stand overnight.
2. To make the pastry, sift the flour and a pinch of salt into a bowl. Dice the butter into the flour and rub in (cut in), then mix to a dough with the water. Roll out the dough on a floured surface and line a buttered 22cm/8½ inch flan dish or tart pan. Prick the base lightly with a fork and bake blind in a preheated moderately hot oven (200°C/400°F, Gas Mark 6) for about 10 minutes, until the pastry has begun to form a slight crust.
3. To make the filling, mix together the eggs and the remaining sugar in a bowl. Add the flour and orange rind and then stir in the cream.
4. Place the rhubarb in the pastry case and cover with the filling. Return to the oven for 30 minutes.
5. Melt the jelly with the water and use to brush over the tart. Serve hot or cold.

Tarte à la Bouillie
(Custard Tart)

This tart was traditionally eaten by farming families in the earlier part of this century. It was difficult in those days to make regular shopping expeditions and the ingredients in this recipe were usually to hand.

METRIC/IMPERIAL	AMERICAN
Pastry:	**Pastry:**
200g/7oz plain flour	1¾ cups all-purpose flour
salt	salt
100g/3½oz butter	½ cup butter
3 tablespoons cold water	3 tablespoons cold water
Filling:	**Filling:**
40g/1½oz plain flour	⅓ cup all-purpose flour
40g/1½oz caster sugar	3 tablespoons sugar
2 eggs	2 eggs
500ml/16 fl oz milk	2 cups milk
vanilla essence	vanilla
25g/1oz butter	2 tablespoons butter

1. To make the pastry, sift the flour and salt into a bowl. Dice the butter into the flour and rub in (cut in), then mix to a dough with the cold water. Roll out the dough on a floured surface and line a deep 22cm/8½ inch flan dish or tart pan. Prick the base lightly with a fork.
2. To make the filling, mix together the flour and sugar and beat in the eggs until the mixture is smooth and free from lumps. Gradually stir in the milk, keeping the consistency very smooth. Bring to the boil in a medium saucepan stirring constantly. Remove from the heat and add a few drops of vanilla essence. Add the butter while the milk is still fairly hot and stir until it has melted.
3. Pour this custard-like mixture into the pastry case and bake in a preheated moderately hot oven (200°C/400°F, Gas Mark 6) for about 30 minutes, until completely cooked. Serve cold.

◁ *Tarte à la Rhubarbe*

Claudine

Claudine and her writer husband are rarely tempted away from their glamorous apartment. They have all they want at home. Even fine wine and a delicious tart may have to wait their turn while the master and mistress build up an appetite.

Tarte aux Bananes à la Noix de Coco

(Banana and Coconut Tart)

METRIC/IMPERIAL	AMERICAN
Pastry:	**Pastry:**
200g/7oz plain flour	1¾ cups all-purpose flour
salt	salt
100g/3½oz butter	½ cup butter
3 tablespoons cold water	3 tablespoons cold water
Filling:	**Filling:**
7 tablespoons milk	7 tablespoons milk
75g/3oz caster sugar	6 tablespoons sugar
100g/3½oz dessicated coconut	1 cup shredded coconut
2 eggs, beaten	2 eggs, beaten
1 tablespoon rum	1 tablespoon rum
5 bananas, sliced	5 bananas, sliced
juice of 1 lemon	juice of 1 lemon
Syrup:	**Syrup:**
1 tablespoon rum	1 tablespoon rum
4 tablespoons sugar	4 tablespoons sugar
To decorate:	**To decorate:**
150ml/¼ pint double cream, whipped	⅔ cup heavy cream, whipped
8 maraschino cherries	8 maraschino cherries

1. To make the pastry, sift the flour and a pinch of salt into a bowl. Dice the butter into the flour and rub in (cut in), then mix to a dough with the cold water. Roll out the dough on a floured surface and line a buttered 22cm/8½ inch flan dish or tart pan. Prick the base lightly with a fork and bake blind in a preheated moderately hot oven (200°C/400°F, Gas Mark 6) for about 15 minutes, until the pastry has begun to form a slight crust. Remove the foil from the pastry and continue to bake for a further 10 minutes until completely baked.
2. To make the filling, boil the milk in a small pan and leave to cool slightly. Mix together the sugar and the coconut, then stir in the beaten eggs. Add the milk, stirring, then return to the pan and thicken over a low heat, stirring constantly. Add the rum and leave the mixture to cool.
3. Toss the banana slices in the lemon juice; strain off the juice and reserve it.
4. In another small pan mix the rum, sugar and the strained lemon juice from the bananas. Heat the mixture over a low heat until the sugar dissolves, then boil to form a thick syrup.
5. Pour the coconut mixture into the pastry case. Arrange the bananas over the top and pour over the syrup. Decorate with swirls of cream and the cherries. Serve at room temperature.

Tourte aux Poires

(Pear Torte)

METRIC/IMPERIAL	AMERICAN
2 eggs	2 eggs
salt	salt
125g/4oz caster sugar	½ cup sugar
75g/3oz self-raising flour	¾ cup self-rising flour
25g/1oz cornflour	¼ cup cornstarch
1½ teaspoons baking powder	1½ teaspoons baking powder
75g/3oz butter, melted	6 tablespoons butter, melted
3 pears, cut in 4 lengthways	3 pears, cut in 4 lengthways
1 tablespoon brown sugar	1 tablespoon brown sugar

1. Beat together the eggs and a pinch of salt. Add the sugar and beat until pale and frothy. Sift in the flour, cornflour (cornstarch) and baking powder and beat well. Whisk in the melted butter.
2. Pour the mixture into a buttered 22cm/8½ inch round ovenproof dish. Arrange the pear quarters on the top in a circular pattern. Sprinkle with brown sugar.
3. Bake in a preheated moderately hot oven (200°C/400°F, Gas Mark 6) for 35 minutes. Serve hot or cold.

Tarte aux Bananes à la Noix de Coco ▷

38

The Commonest Tart of All

A plain or dowdy appearance may often hide an exciting and intriguing character. So it is with the apple tart, undoubtedly the most popular and versatile tart of them all. Some are glazed and crunchy, others are alcoholic, but they all turn out to be surprisingly spicy little numbers.

Alison

A rustic beauty, glowing with health, Alison is responsible for the welfare of the farm-workers on her father's farm, and is kept fully occupied, especially at hay-making time.

Bande de Pommes

(Apple Strip)

METRIC/IMPERIAL
250g/8oz frozen puff pastry
1 egg yolk, beaten
1kg/2lb apples
2 tablespoons water
1 tablespoon lemon juice
Pastry cream:
1 quantity pastry cream, see
  Tartelettes aux Abricots,
  page 21
Glaze:
3 tablespoons apricot jam
1 tablespoon water

AMERICAN
8oz frozen puff pastry
1 egg yolk, beaten
2lb apples
2 tablespoons water
1 tablespoon lemon juice
Pastry cream:
1 quantity pastry cream, see
  Tartelettes aux Abricots,
  page 21
Glaze:
3 tablespoons apricot jam
1 tablespoon water

1. Defrost and roll out the pastry into a rectangle 12cm/5 inches wide. Sprinkle lightly with flour and fold in half lengthwise. Cut a 1cm/½ inch band from around the three open edges. Open out the rectangle and roll again so that it is 2cm/1 inch wider and longer. Place on a dampened baking sheet, prick with a fork and dampen the edges. Open the band of pastry and press on to the rectangle to make a border. Brush the border with a little beaten egg yolk. Bake in a preheated moderately hot oven (200°C/400°F, Gas Mark 6) for 10 minutes.
2. Peel and slice the apples thinly. Cook a quarter of them with the water until they have formed a smooth purée. Meanwhile, prevent the uncooked apple slices from turning brown by turning them in the lemon juice.
3. Spread the pastry cream evenly over the uncooked pastry base. Cover this with a layer of apple purée, then arrange the apple slices in a fish scale pattern over the purée – start at the centre and work out. Brush the pastry edges with the leftover egg yolk.
4. Reduce the heat to 180°C/350°F, Gas Mark 4, and cook for a further 10 minutes. In a small pan melt the apricot jam in the water then boil until smooth, stirring with a wooden spoon. Brush this over the apple slices. Serve hot or cold.

Tarte aux Pommes à la Cannelle

(Apple Tart with Cinnamon)

METRIC/IMPERIAL
Pastry:
200g/7oz plain flour
salt
100g/3½oz butter
3 tablespoons cold water
Filling:
750g/1½lb apples
juice of 1 lemon
1½ tablespoons sultanas
25g/1oz sugar
¼ teaspoon ground cinnamon
¼ teaspoon grated nutmeg
2 cloves, ground
75g/3oz brown sugar
75g/3oz plain flour
grated rind of 1 lemon
75g/3oz butter, softened

AMERICAN
Pastry:
1¾ cups all-purpose flour
salt
½ cup butter
3 tablespoons cold water
Filling:
1½lb apples
juice of 1 lemon
1½ tablespoons golden raisins
2 tablespoons sugar
¼ teaspoon ground cinnamon
¼ teaspoon grated nutmeg
2 cloves, ground
½ cup brown sugar
¾ cup all-purpose flour
grated rind of 1 lemon
6 tablespoons butter, softened

1. For the pastry, sift the flour and a pinch of salt into a bowl. Dice the butter into the flour and rub in (cut in), then mix to a dough with the cold water. Roll out the dough on a floured surface and line a buttered 22cm/8½ inch flan dish or tart pan. Prick the base lightly with a fork.
2. For the filling, peel, core and slice the apples and toss them in the lemon juice. Arrange them in the unbaked pastry case.
3. Mix the sultanas (golden raisins), sugar, cinnamon, nutmeg and cloves and sprinkle them over the apples.
4. To make the topping, mix the brown sugar, flour and lemon rind in a bowl. Using 2 knives cut the soft butter until it resembles coarse breadcrumbs. Sprinkle over the apples and bake in a preheated hot oven (220°C/425°F, Gas Mark 7) for 15 minutes. Reduce the heat to 160°C/325°F, Gas Mark 3, and bake for a further 30 minutes. Serve hot or cold.

Bande de Pommes ▷

42

Marie-Claude

*Marie-Claude abandoned her chosen career as a chef catering
for hundreds to cater only for the needs of her husband, Paul.
Their little girl stays with Granny when Marie-Claude wants
to lay on something special.*

Tarte aux Pommes à l'Orange

(Apple and Orange Tart)

METRIC/IMPERIAL	AMERICAN
Pastry:	**Pastry:**
200g/7oz plain flour	1¾ cups all-purpose flour
salt	salt
100g/3½oz butter	½ cup butter
3 tablespoons cold water	3 tablespoons cold water
Filling:	**Filling:**
1kg/2lb red eating apples	2lb red eating apples
1 orange	1 orange
25g/1oz butter	2 tablespoons butter
1 tablespoon water	1 tablespoon water
25g/1oz sugar	2 tablespoons sugar
2 tablespoons apricot jam	2 tablespoons apricot jam

1. Sift the flour and a pinch of salt into a bowl. Dice the butter into the flour and rub in (cut in), then mix to a dough with the cold water. Roll out the dough on a floured surface and line a buttered 22cm/8½ inch flan dish or tart pan. Prick the base lightly with a fork and bake blind in a preheated moderately hot oven (200°C/400°F, Gas Mark 6) for about 10 minutes, until the pastry has begun to form a slight crust.
2. For the filling, slice the apples, leaving on the skin. Grate the rind of the orange and squeeze out its juice. Melt the butter in a pan over a low heat, then add the water, orange rind and juice and the sugar. Still on the heat, toss the apple slices in the mixture. When they have just begun to soften remove them from the pan with a slotted spoon. Arrange the slices in the pastry case in overlapping concentric circles.
3. Boil the apricot jam in the pan with the apple and orange juice mixture until it is smooth – add a little extra water if necessary. Pour this glaze over the fruit and bake for 20 minutes. Serve hot or cold.

◁ *Tarte aux Pommes Basquaise*

Tarte aux Pommes Basquaise

(Basque Apple Tart)

METRIC/IMPERIAL	AMERICAN
Pastry:	**Pastry:**
200g/7oz plain flour	1¾ cups all-purpose flour
salt	salt
100g/3½oz butter	½ cup butter
1 egg yolk	1 egg yolk
2 tablespoons cold water	2 tablespoons cold water
Filling:	**Filling:**
6 to 8 eating apples	6 to 8 eating apples
juice of 1 lemon	juice of 1 lemon
75g/3oz butter	⅓ cup butter
100g/3½oz caster sugar	½ cup sugar
1 tablespoon ground cinnamon	1 tablespoon ground cinnamon

1. To make the pastry, sift the flour and a pinch of salt into a bowl. Dice the butter into the flour and rub in (cut in). Stir in the egg yolk with a fork, then mix to a dough with the cold water. Roll out the dough on a floured surface and line a buttered 22cm/8½ inch flan dish or tart pan. Prick the base lightly with a fork and bake blind in a preheated moderately hot oven (200°C/400°F, Gas Mark 6) for about 20 minutes, until the pastry is fully cooked.
2. For the filling, peel the apples and slice them thickly. Toss the slices in the lemon juice. Melt 50g/2oz (½ cup) butter in a shallow pan and lightly sauté the apples with the lemon juice, 75g/3oz (⅓ cup) sugar and the cinnamon. Cook until the apples are soft but not disintegrating.
3. Remove the slices from the pan and reserve the juice. Arrange in the pastry case in overlapping concentric circles.
4. Sprinkle the apples with the remaining sugar and the rest of the butter cut into knobs. Heat the grill (broiler) to high.
5. Boil up the reserved apple juice in a small pan until it is thick and syrupy and spoon this over the fruit.
6. Place the tart under the grill (broiler) until the topping has caramelized. It may be necessary to protect the pastry edges from burning with crumpled aluminium foil.

Judith

*Judith is an animal lover, and lives in the heart of the country with
a houseful of permanently pregnant cats. Both she and husband Jules
enjoy the natural things of life more and more as the years go by.*

Tarte au Calvados Meringué

(Calvados Meringue Tart)

METRIC/IMPERIAL	AMERICAN
Pastry:	*Pastry:*
200g/7oz plain flour	*1¾ cups all-purpose flour*
salt	*salt*
100g/3½oz butter	*½ cup butter*
3 tablespoons cold milk	*3 tablespoons cold milk*
Filling:	*Filling:*
25g/1oz butter	*2 tablespoons butter*
1kg/2lb eating apples, peeled and sliced	*2lb eating apples, peeled and sliced*
3 tablespoons Calvados	*3 tablespoons applejack*
2 eggs, separated	*2 eggs, separated*
2 tablespoons caster sugar	*2 tablespoons sugar*
1 tablespoon cornflour	*1 tablespoon cornstarch*
150ml/¼ pint milk	*⅔ cup milk*
50g/2oz sifted icing sugar	*½ cup sifted confectioners' sugar*

1. Sift the flour and a pinch of salt into a bowl. Dice the butter into the flour and rub in (cut in), then mix to a dough with the milk. Leave to rest in the refrigerator for 20 minutes before rolling out on a floured surface. Line a buttered 22cm/ 8½ inch flan dish or tart pan. Prick the base lightly with a fork and bake blind in a preheated moderately hot oven (200°C/ 400°F, Gas Mark 6) for about 10 minutes.
2. Melt the butter in a frying pan (skillet) and sauté the apples until they are soft. Hold 1 tablespoon of the Calvados (applejack) over a flame until it is hot, then light it with a match and pour it over the apples to flambé them.
3. Make a pastry cream by stirring together the egg yolks, caster sugar and cornflour (cornstarch) in a very small pan. Add a little of the milk and beat until smooth. Gradually add the remaining milk and stir over a low heat until it is smooth and thick. Stir in another tablespoon of the Calvados. Spread this evenly over the pastry case. Arrange the apples over the pastry cream, keeping the surface level.
4. Whisk the egg whites until stiff, stir in the icing sugar (confectioners' sugar) and continue to whisk until the whites stand in peaks. Spread this over the apples, fluffing up the whites with a fork.
5. Bake in the oven for 8 minutes until the meringue has begun to colour. Remove from the oven and sprinkle with the remaining Calvados (applejack). Serve hot.

Tarte Tatin

(Traditional Upside-Down Apple Tart)

METRIC/IMPERIAL	AMERICAN
Pastry:	*Pastry:*
200g/7oz plain flour	*1¾ cups all-purpose flour*
salt	*salt*
100g/3½oz butter	*½ cup butter*
1 egg, beaten	*1 egg, beaten*
2 tablespoons cold water	*2 tablespoons cold water*
Filling:	*Filling:*
1kg/2lb Golden Delicious apples, peeled	*2lb Golden Delicious apples, peeled*
175g/6oz caster sugar	*¾ cup sugar*
15g/½oz butter	*1 tablespoon butter*

1. To make the pastry, sift the flour and a pinch of salt into a bowl. Dice the butter into the flour and rub in (cut in). Stir in the beaten egg, then mix to a dough with the water. Refrigerate the dough for 1 hour then roll it out on a floured surface.
2. For the filling, cut the apples into thick slices. Butter a 20cm/8 inch round cake tin and sprinkle with half the sugar.
3. Coat the apple slices in the remaining sugar and place them in the tin. Dot the apples with the butter.
4. Cover the apples with the pastry dough, tucking it down the sides of the tin. Hold the tin over a medium flame for 3 minutes, when the sugar will caramelize in the heat, then bake in a preheated moderately hot oven (200°C/400°F, Gas Mark 6) for 30 minutes. When cooked, turn the tart out of the tin, so that the fruit is on the surface. Serve warm.

Tarte au Calvados Meringué ▷

46

Jeanne

Jeanne is a highly successful business executive, but in every spare moment she heads for her thatched cottage in the country, strips off her smart clothes and climbs into wellington boots to indulge in more pleasurable, rural pastimes.

Tarte aux Pommes aux Groseilles

(Apple Tart with Redcurrant)

METRIC/IMPERIAL	AMERICAN
Pastry:	**Pastry:**
200g/7oz plain flour	1¾ cups all-purpose flour
salt	salt
100g/3½oz butter	½ cup butter
3 tablespoons cold water	3 tablespoons cold water
Filling:	**Filling:**
1kg/2lb red apples	2lb red apples
6 tablespoons sugar	6 tablespoons sugar
3 tablespoons water	3 tablespoons water
15g/½oz butter	1 tablespoon butter
1 tablespoon Calvados	1 tablespoon applejack
Glaze:	**Glaze:**
2 tablespoons redcurrant jelly	2 tablespoons redcurrant jelly
1 tablespoon water	1 tablespoon water

1. To make the pastry, sift the flour and a pinch of salt into a bowl. Dice the butter into the flour and rub in (cut in), then mix to a dough with the cold water. Roll out the dough on a floured surface and use it to line a buttered 22cm/8½ inch flan dish or tart pan. Prick the base lightly with a fork.
2. For the filling, peel, core and slice all the apples but two. Cook the slices with 4 tablespoons sugar, the water and butter until they have made a thick, smooth purée. Pour this into the pastry case.
3. Core and slice the remaining apples and toss them in the Calvados (applejack). Arrange them in a circular pattern over the purée and sprinkle with the remaining sugar.
4. Bake the tart in a preheated moderately hot oven (200°C/400°F, Gas Mark 6) for 30 minutes.
5. Meanwhile boil the redcurrant jelly and water in a small pouring saucepan. Stir with a wooden spoon until smooth.
6. Remove the cooked tart from the oven and slowly swirl the hot, red glaze over it in a spiral pattern.

◁ *Tarte aux Pommes aux Groseilles*

Tarte aux Pommes Amandine

(Apple Tart with Almonds)

METRIC/IMPERIAL	AMERICAN
Pastry:	**Pastry:**
200g/7oz plain flour	1¾ cups all-purpose flour
salt	salt
65g/2½oz butter	5 tablespoons butter
65g/2½oz caster sugar	5 tablespoons sugar
1 egg, beaten	1 egg, beaten
3 tablespoons cold water	3 tablespoons cold water
Filling:	**Filling:**
65g/2½oz butter	5 tablespoons butter
1 tablespoon water	1 tablespoon water
6 Golden Delicious apples, peeled, cored and sliced	6 Golden Delicious apples, peeled, cored and sliced
75g/3oz ground almonds	¾ cup ground almonds
100g/3½oz caster sugar	scant ½ cup sugar
3 eggs, 2 separated	3 eggs, 2 separated
2 tablespoons plain flour	2 tablespoons all-purpose flour
2 tablespoons Cointreau	2 tablespoons Cointreau
4 tablespoons icing sugar, to decorate	4 tablespoons confectioners' sugar, to decorate

1. Sift the flour and a pinch of salt into a bowl. Dice the butter and rub in (cut in). Using a wooden spoon, stir in the sugar and then the beaten egg. Mix to a dough with the water and leave in the refrigerator to rest for 20 minutes.
2. Meanwhile, melt the butter for the filling, add the water and lightly sauté the apples for 2 to 3 minutes.
3. Mix together the ground almonds and caster sugar. Beat in the whole egg and 2 yolks, then the flour and liqueur. In a separate bowl whisk the egg whites.
4. Roll out the pastry on a floured surface and line a 22cm/8½ inch flan dish or tart pan. Prick well with a fork. Arrange the apples in the unbaked pastry case. Fold the egg whites into the almond mixture and pour over the apples.
5. Bake in a preheated moderately hot oven (200°C/400°F, Gas Mark 6) for 35 minutes. Sprinkle with sugar.

Françoise

Françoise remembers her schooldays with great fondness.
She loves tarting herself up in her old uniform, and teacher husband
Etienne certainly doesn't object. "An apple", or in this case
"apple tart, for the teacher" sweetens him up even more.

Tarte aux Pommes Bretonne

(Breton Apple Tart)

The round tart can also be prepared in a square dish and cut into rectangular portions. This method is most effective if the lattice work is made with very fine strips of pastry.

METRIC/IMPERIAL	AMERICAN
Pastry:	**Pastry:**
200g/7oz plain flour	1¾ cups all-purpose flour
salt	salt
100g/3½oz butter	½ cup butter
1 tablespoon sugar	1 tablespoon sugar
3 tablespoons cold water	3 tablespoons cold water
Filling:	**Filling:**
1kg/2lb Golden Delicious apples	2lb Golden Delicious apples
40g/1½oz sugar	3 tablespoons sugar
40g/1½oz butter	3 tablespoons butter
1 egg yolk, beaten	1 egg yolk, beaten

1. To make the pastry, sift the flour and a pinch of salt into a bowl. Dice the butter into the flour and rub in (cut in). Stir in the sugar and mix to a dough with the cold water. Leave the dough to rest in the refrigerator for 20 minutes.
2. Remove the dough from the refrigerator and work it a little, using your hands. Flatten slightly, fold into 4 and repeat. Roll out onto a floured surface and line a buttered 22cm/8½ inch flan dish or tart pan. Reserve the leftover dough. Bake blind in a preheated hot oven (220°C/425°F, Gas Mark 7) for about 10 minutes.
3. For the filling, first peel and slice the apples. Arrange them in the pastry case in overlapping concentric circles. Sprinkle with the sugar and knobs of butter.
4. Roll out the reserved pastry dough, cut it into long thin strips and lay them across the tart to form a lattice design. Brush the strips with the beaten egg yolk.
5. Return to the oven for 30 to 35 minutes. Serve this striking tart hot or cold.

Tarte aux Pommes Pas Chère

(Economical Apple Tart)

METRIC/IMPERIAL	AMERICAN
Pastry:	**Pastry:**
200g/7oz plain flour	1¾ cups all-purpose flour
salt	salt
100g/3½oz butter	½ cup butter
3 tablespoons cold water	3 tablespoons cold water
Filling:	**Filling:**
1kg/2lb eating apples	2lb eating apples
lemon juice	lemon juice
3 tablespoons water	3 tablespoons water
about 50g/2oz sugar	about ¼ cup sugar

1. To make the pastry, sift the flour and a pinch of salt into a bowl. Dice the butter into the flour and rub in (cut in), then mix to a dough with the water. Roll out the dough on a floured surface and line a buttered 22cm/8½ inch flan dish or tart pan. Prick the base lightly with a fork and bake blind in a preheated moderately hot oven (200°C/400°F, Gas Mark 6) for about 10 minutes, until the pastry has begun to form a slight crust.
2. For the filling, peel and core the apples and reserve two; to prevent them going brown, set them in a bowl of water that has been acidulated with a little lemon juice. Chop the remaining apples and cook them slowly with the water and sugar to taste until they have become a smooth purée.
3. Spread the purée over the base of the tart and reserve 2 tablespoons for the glaze.
4. Slice the remaining apples evenly and arrange them overlapping in a circular pattern over the purée. Brush the slices with the extra purée and sprinkle the top with a little extra sugar.
5. Bake the tart for 30 minutes and serve hot or cold.

Tarte aux Pommes Bretonne ▷

A Piece of Hot Stuff

This particular breed of tart comes in many guises. Whether spicy tomato, asparagus, crab or a delicious quiche, the savoury tart will always provide a little of what you fancy. A tart on its own is a tempting starter, or partnered with salad or vegetables makes an appetizing main course. And tarts dressed up can be the centre of attention at any festive occasion.

Estelle

*Estelle loves staying in hotels in out of the way places with out of
the ordinary people, and a simple meal for two in a hotel bedroom
adds spice to an already piquant situation.*

Tarte aux Poireaux
(Leek Tart)

METRIC/IMPERIAL	AMERICAN
Pastry:	**Pastry:**
200g/7oz plain flour	*1¾ cups all-purpose flour*
salt	*salt*
100g/3½oz butter	*½ cup butter*
1 egg yolk	*1 egg yolk*
2 tablespoons cold water	*2 tablespoons cold water*
Filling:	**Filling:**
50g/2oz butter	*¼ cup butter*
6 leeks, finely sliced	*6 leeks, finely sliced*
freshly ground black pepper	*freshly ground black pepper*
2 tablespoons plain flour	*2 tablespoons all-purpose flour*
120ml/4fl oz milk	*½ cup milk*
3 tablespoons double cream	*3 tablespoons heavy cream*
2 eggs, beaten	*2 eggs, beaten*
50g/2oz Cheddar, grated	*½ cup grated Cheddar*

1. To make the pastry, sift the flour and a pinch of salt into a
bowl. Dice the butter into the flour and rub in (cut in). Stir in
the egg yolk with a fork. Mix to a dough with the water. Roll
out the dough on a floured surface and line a buttered 22cm/
8½ inch flan dish or tart pan. Prick the base lightly with a fork
and bake blind in a preheated moderately hot oven (200°C/
400°F, Gas Mark 6) for about 10 minutes.
2. To make the filling, melt half of the butter in a pan and
sauté the leeks, then cover them and simmer for 10 minutes.
Pour over 250ml/8fl oz (1 cup) boiling water. When the leeks
are cooked, drain, reserving the liquid.
3. Melt the remaining butter in a small pan, add the flour and
mix with a wooden spoon to form a roux. Cook, stirring, for a
few minutes then add the milk and the leek water and keep
stirring over a low heat until the sauce is smooth. Bring to the
boil and cook for 3 minutes. Remove from the heat and stir in
seasoning, the cream, beaten eggs and half the cheese.
4. Line the pastry case with the leeks and pour over the sauce.
Sprinkle with remaining cheese and black pepper.
5. Bake for 20 minutes and serve hot with green salad.

Tarte aux Carrottes et à l'Orange
(Carrot and Orange Tart)

METRIC/IMPERIAL	AMERICAN
Pastry:	**Pastry:**
200g/7oz plain flour	*1¾ cups all-purpose flour*
salt	*salt*
100g/3½oz butter	*½ cup butter*
3 tablespoons cold water	*3 tablespoons cold water*
Filling:	**Filling:**
1kg/2lb carrots, peeled and sliced	*2lb carrots, peeled and sliced*
50g/2oz butter, diced	*¼ cup butter, diced*
120ml/4fl oz double cream	*½ cup heavy cream*
2 oranges	*2 oranges*
salt	*salt*
freshly ground black pepper	*freshly ground black pepper*

1. To make the pastry, sift the flour and a pinch of salt into a
bowl. Dice the butter into the flour and rub in (cut in) then
mix to a dough with the water. Roll out the dough on a floured
surface and line a buttered 22cm/8½ inch flan dish or tart pan.
Prick the base lightly with a fork and bake blind in a preheated
moderately hot oven (200°C/400°F, Gas Mark 6) for about 20
minutes, until the pastry is completely cooked.
2. To make the filling, cook the carrots in a pan of salted
water and purée them in a blender or food processor.
3. Fold in the butter and the cream.
4. Grate the rind of one orange and add it to the purée with
its juice. Adjust the seasoning if necessary.
5. Pour the carrot and orange purée into the pastry case and
return the tart to the oven for a few minutes until it has risen
and developed a glaze over the surface.
6. Cut the rind of the remaining orange into long strips with a
sharp knife or grater. Sprinkle these 'Julienne' strips over the
tart. Serve this unusual tart with a nutty salad and hot
potatoes of some kind.

*Tarte aux Carrottes et à l'Orange (top)
and Tarte aux Poireaux (below)* ▷

Dominique

*Dominique and her husband are both fans of the fifties,
and often give parties for like-minded friends who love dressing up
in stilettos and net. But when it comes to enjoying themselves,
they're very much people of today.*

Tarte aux Champignons

(Mushroom Tart)

METRIC/IMPERIAL	AMERICAN
Pastry:	**Pastry:**
200g/7oz plain flour	1¾ cups all-purpose flour
salt	salt
100g/3½oz butter	½ cup butter
3 tablespoons cold water	3 tablespoons cold water
Filling:	**Filling:**
300g/10oz mushrooms, sliced	2½ cups sliced mushrooms
15g/½oz butter	1 tablespoon butter
1 egg	1 egg
300ml/10fl oz double cream	1¼ cups heavy cream
75g/3oz Gruyère, grated	¾ cup grated Gruyère
1 tablespoon cornflour	1 tablespoon cornstarch
freshly ground black pepper	freshly ground black pepper
coriander sprig to garnish	coriander sprig to garnish

1. To make the pastry, sift the flour and a pinch of salt into a bowl. Dice the butter into the flour and rub in (cut in), then mix to a dough with the water. Roll out the dough on a floured surface and line a buttered 22cm/8½ inch flan dish or tart pan. Prick the base with a fork and bake blind in a preheated moderately hot oven (200°C/400°F, Gas Mark 6) for about 10 minutes.
2. For the filling, fry the sliced mushrooms in the butter until cooked. Remove them from the pan with a slotted spoon and distribute them evenly over the pastry case.
3. Beat together the egg, cream, cheese and cornflour (cornstarch). Add salt and pepper to taste – I find that mushrooms like a lot of pepper. Pour this mixture over the mushrooms.
4. Return the tart to the oven for 30 minutes, then reduce the oven temperature to 180°C/350°F, Gas Mark 4, and bake for a further 15 minutes. Garnish with a coriander sprig and serve with a tossed green salad.

◁ *Tarte aux Champignons*

Tarte au Fromage – Nature

(Plain Cheese Tart)

METRIC/IMPERIAL	AMERICAN
Pastry:	**Pastry:**
200g/7oz plain flour	1¾ cups all-purpose flour
salt	salt
100g/3½oz butter	½ cup butter
1 heaped teaspoon sugar	1 heaped teaspoon sugar
3 tablespoons cold water	3 tablespoons cold water
Filling:	**Filling:**
150g/5oz Comté or Gruyère, grated	1¼ cups grated Comté or Gruyère
3 eggs	3 eggs
150ml/¼ pint double cream	⅔ cup heavy cream
250ml/8fl oz milk	1 cup milk
freshly ground black pepper	freshly ground black pepper
grated nutmeg	grated nutmeg

1. Sift the flour and a pinch of salt into a bowl. Dice the butter into the flour and rub in (cut in). Stir in the sugar. Dominique always adds sugar to both sweet and savoury pastry because it gives the cooked crust a rich golden colour. Mix the flour and fat to a dough with the water. Roll out onto a floured surface and use it to line a 22cm/8½ inch buttered flan dish or tart pan. Prick well with a fork and then chill for 30 minutes.
2. As the pastry has been chilled, it is not necessary to cover it with aluminium foil weighted with dried beans before you bake it blind. Bake in a preheated moderately hot oven (200°C/400°F, Gas Mark 6) for 5 to 8 minutes.
3. For the filling, fill the pastry case with the grated Comté or Gruyère and level the surface.
4. Beat the eggs with a fork in a medium bowl. Add the cream and continue to beat. Add the milk, and salt, pepper and nutmeg to taste. Beat well and pour evenly over the cheese. Check that no cheese is visible through the milk mixture.
5. Raise the oven temperature to 220°C/425°F, Gas Mark 7, and bake the tart on the bottom shelf for 20 minutes until golden. Serve immediately.

Alvina

Alvina and her husband, le Comte, together manage their beautiful fourteenth-century château in the Loire, complete with acres of thriving vineyards. Alvina insists on wine with dinner, because she knows that the perfect accompaniment to a tart is vintage refreshment.

Tarte au Saumon

(Salmon Tart)

METRIC/IMPERIAL	AMERICAN
Pastry:	**Pastry:**
200g/7oz plain flour	1¾ cups all-purpose flour
salt	salt
100g/3½oz butter	scant ½ cup butter
3 tablespoons cold water	3 tablespoons cold water
Filling:	**Filling:**
1 × 150g/5oz can salmon	1 × 5oz can salmon
125g/4oz mushrooms, sliced	1 cup sliced mushrooms
1 tablespoon butter	1 tablespoon butter
3 hard boiled eggs, sliced	3 hard-cooked eggs, sliced
6 black olives, halved	6 pitted ripe olives, halved
Béchamel Sauce:	**Béchamel Sauce:**
25g/1oz butter	2 tablespoons butter
25g/1oz flour	¼ cup all-purpose flour
300ml/½ pint milk	1¼ cups milk
freshly ground black pepper	freshly ground black pepper

1. To make the pastry, sift the flour and a pinch of salt into a bowl. Dice the butter into the flour and rub in (cut in). Stir in the cold water and mix to a dough. Roll out onto a floured surface and use it to line a buttered 22cm/8½ inch flan dish or tart pan. Prick the base well with a fork and refrigerate for 30 minutes.
2. Bake without covering of any kind in a preheated moderately hot oven (200°C/400°F, Gas Mark 6) for 5 minutes.
3. For the filling, drain the salmon and distribute it evenly over the base of the pastry case. Lightly fry the mushrooms in the butter. Scatter them over the salmon. Arrange the egg slices on top and dot the surface with olives.
4. For the Béchamel sauce, melt the butter in a small pan, stir in the flour and cook for a couple of minutes. Gradually stir in the milk, bring to the boil and cook until the sauce has thickened, stirring continually. Add salt and pepper to taste.
5. Pour the sauce into the tart case and bake towards the bottom of the oven for 20 to 30 minutes. Serve hot or cold.

Tarte aux Asperges

(Asparagus Tart)

METRIC/IMPERIAL	AMERICAN
Pastry:	**Pastry:**
200g/7oz plain flour	1¾ cups all-purpose flour
salt	salt
100g/3½oz butter	½ cup butter
3 tablespoons cold water	3 tablespoons cold water
Filling:	**Filling:**
350g/12oz asparagus	¾lb asparagus
75g/3oz Cheddar cheese, grated	¾ cup grated Cheddar cheese
25g/1oz grated Parmesan	¼ cup grated Parmesan
3 eggs	3 eggs
120ml/4fl oz double cream	½ cup heavy cream
freshly ground black pepper	freshly ground black pepper
pinch of grated nutmeg	pinch of grated nutmeg

1. To make the pastry, sift the flour and a pinch of salt into a bowl. Dice the butter into the flour and rub in (cut in), then mix to a dough with the water. Roll out the dough on a floured surface and line a buttered 22cm/8½ inch flan dish or tart pan. Prick the base with a fork and bake blind in a preheated moderately hot oven (200°C/400°F, Gas Mark 6) for 10 minutes.
2. To prepare the filling, first wash the asparagus and trim away the woody ends of the stalks, so that all the spears are the same length. Bring a shallow pan of salted water to the boil and cook the asparagus over a low heat for about 15 minutes.
3. Mix together the grated cheeses and use a third to cover the base of the pastry case. Arrange the asparagus on top.
4. Beat together the eggs, cream, remaining cheese and seasonings and pour over the asparagus. Reduce the oven temperature to 190°C/375°F, Gas Mark 5, and bake the tart for just over 30 minutes until the filling has set.
5. Finally, protect the pastry crust with aluminium foil and place under a hot grill (broiler) for a minute or two.

Tarte aux Asperges ▷

58

Renée

Renée, invited by friends to stay the summer in St Tropez, very quickly took to sunbathing as the locals do. Hardly surprising, since many of the best French tarts go topless.

Quiche au Bacon

(Bacon Quiche)

If you are apprehensive about trying this pastry then use the recipe from another tart in the collection. But Renée's pastry is exceptional; the colour of caramel, it melts in the mouth.

METRIC/IMPERIAL	AMERICAN
Pastry:	*Pastry:*
200g/7oz plain flour	*1¾ cups all-purpose flour*
salt	*salt*
2 tablespoons double cream	*2 tablespoons heavy cream*
1 egg yolk	*1 egg yolk*
Filling:	*Filling:*
200g/7oz lean belly pork, cubed	*1 cup cubed lean fresh pork sides*
25g/1oz butter	*2 tablespoons butter*
4 eggs	*4 eggs*
120ml/4fl oz single cream	*½ cup light cream*
125g/4oz Gruyère, grated	*1 cup grated Gruyère*
freshly ground black pepper	*freshly ground black pepper*

1. Sift the flour and a pinch of salt into a bowl. Stir in the cream and the yolk with a fork and form into a dough. If the consistency is too dry then add a little more cream. Roll out the dough on a floured surface and line a large 25cm/10 inch flan dish or tart pan.
2. To make the filling, fry the cubed pork in the butter until it has cooked through. Distribute it in the base of the uncooked pastry case.
3. Beat together the eggs, cream, Gruyère, salt and pepper and pour over the pork.
4. Bake in a preheated moderately hot oven (200°C/400°F, Gas Mark 6) for 30 minutes then reduce the heat to 180°C/350°F, Gas Mark 4 and cook for a further 10 minutes.
5. Renée always serves this rich tart hot and free from garnish of any kind, as an excellent and satisfying hors d'oeuvre.

◁ *Tarte à la Viande et à la Sauge*

Tarte à la Viande et à la Sauge

(Sage and Meat Tart)

METRIC/IMPERIAL	AMERICAN
Pastry:	*Pastry:*
200g/7oz plain flour	*1¾ cups all-purpose flour*
salt	*salt*
100g/3½oz butter	*½ cup butter*
3 tablespoons cold water	*3 tablespoons cold water*
Filling:	*Filling:*
15g/½oz butter	*1 tablespoon butter*
1 large onion, sliced	*1 large onion, sliced*
1 clove garlic, crushed	*1 clove garlic, crushed*
200g/7oz pork sausagemeat	*1 scant cup pork sausagemeat*
200g/7oz minced beef	*1 scant cup ground beef, firmly packed*
3 tomatoes	*3 tomatoes*
1 whole egg, beaten	*1 whole egg, beaten*
½ teaspoon dried sage	*½ teaspoon dried sage*
freshly ground black pepper	*freshly ground black pepper*
1 egg white	*1 egg white*
4 or 5 leaves fresh sage	*4 or 5 leaves fresh sage*

1. To make the pastry, sift the flour and a pinch of salt into a bowl. Dice the butter into the flour and rub in (cut in) then mix to a dough with the water. Roll out the dough on a floured surface and line a buttered 22cm/8½ inch flan dish or tart pan. Cut the leftover dough into long strips for the top of the tart.
2. For the filling, heat the butter in a frying pan (skillet) and sauté the onion with the garlic until it has begun to soften. Add the sausagemeat and the minced (ground) beef and brown over quite a high heat for 5 to 7 minutes.
3. Skin and roughly chop the tomatoes and stir them into the meat with the beaten egg, dried sage, salt and pepper to taste.
4. Spread the filling evenly over the unbaked pastry case. Arrange the dough strips across the tart forming a lattice design. Brush these strips with egg white. Place the fresh sage leaves in a pattern between the strips as a garnish.
5. Bake in a preheated moderately hot oven (190°C/375°F, Gas Mark 5) for 40 minutes.

Catherine

*Cathie lives with the son of a restaurateur, well schooled in
the arts of Epicurus. She too has a taste for the finer things of life,
and her beautiful collection of handmade lace enhances many
a romantic rendezvous.*

Tarte aux Courgettes

(Courgette Tart)

METRIC/IMPERIAL
Pastry:
200g/7oz plain flour
salt
125g/4oz butter
3 tablespoons cold water
Filling:
1 tablespoon cooking oil
15g/½oz butter
½ medium onion, chopped
1 clove garlic, crushed
300g/10oz courgettes, sliced
1 egg
75g/3oz Gruyère, grated
120ml/4fl oz milk
freshly ground black pepper

AMERICAN
Pastry:
1¾ cups all-purpose flour
salt
½ cup butter
3 tablespoons cold water
Filling:
1 tablespoon cooking oil
1 tablespoon butter
½ medium onion, chopped
1 clove garlic, crushed
3 cups sliced zucchini
1 egg
¾ cup grated Gruyère
½ cup milk
freshly ground black pepper

1. To make the pastry, sift the flour and a pinch of salt into a bowl. Dice the butter into the flour and rub in (cut in), then mix to a dough with the water. Roll out the dough on a floured surface and use it to line a 22cm/8½ inch buttered flan dish or tart pan. Prick the base with a fork and bake blind in a preheated moderately hot oven (200°C/400°F, Gas Mark 6) for 10 to 15 minutes.
2. For the filling, heat the oil and butter in a frying pan (skillet) and cook the onion and garlic until soft .
3. Add the courgettes (zucchini) to the pan and fry them briskly for a few minutes. Remove them from the pan with a slotted spoon and arrange them evenly over the base of the tart, creating a regular pattern.
4. Whisk together the egg, 50g/2oz (½ cup) cheese, the milk and a little salt and pepper. Pour this evenly over the courgettes (zucchini) and then sprinkle the remaining cheese over.
5. Return the tart to the oven for 30 minutes until it is light golden brown.

Tarte aux Épinards

(Spinach Tart)

METRIC/IMPERIAL
Pastry:
200g/7oz plain flour
salt
100g/3½oz butter
3 tablespoons cold water
Filling:
750g/1½lb cooked spinach, chopped
1 small onion, chopped
grated nutmeg to taste
1 teaspoon lemon juice
100 g/3½oz cream cheese
2 eggs, beaten
3 tablespoons milk
freshly ground black pepper
50g/2oz Cheddar, grated

AMERICAN
Pastry:
1¾ cups all-purpose flour
salt
½ cup butter
3 tablespoons cold water
Filling:
3 cups chopped cooked spinach
1 small onion, chopped
grated nutmeg to taste
1 teaspoon lemon juice
½ cup cream cheese
2 eggs, beaten
3 tablespoons milk
freshly ground black pepper
½ cup grated Cheddar

1. To make the pastry, sift the flour and a pinch of salt into a bowl. Dice the butter into the flour and rub in (cut in) and mix to a dough with the water. Roll out the dough on a floured surface and line a buttered 22cm/8½ inch flan dish or tart pan. Prick the base lightly with a fork and bake blind in a preheated moderately hot oven (200°C/400°F, Gas Mark 6) for about 10 minutes, until the pastry has begun to form a slight crust.
2. To make the filling, mix the well-drained spinach in with the onion, a pinch of nutmeg and the lemon juice. Spread evenly in the pastry case.
3. Beat together the cream cheese, eggs, milk, salt and pepper and pour over the spinach. Sprinkle with the grated cheese.
4. Bake the tart for 30 minutes, then reduce the heat to 180°C/350°F, Gas Mark 4 and continue to cook for a further 10 minutes. Serve warm as a starter, or with mushrooms à la Grècque (see page 94) and a potato salad as a main course.

Tarte aux Courgettes ▷

Angela

*Angela often frequents the local market to sell her wares.
She attracts a great deal of custom, for everything she offers is
fresh and highly original.*

Tarte à l'Oignon
(Onion Tart)

METRIC/IMPERIAL	AMERICAN
Pastry:	**Pastry:**
200g/7oz plain flour	*1¾ cups all-purpose flour*
salt	*salt*
100g/3½oz butter	*½ cup butter*
3 tablespoons cold water	*3 tablespoons cold water*
Filling:	**Filling:**
750g/1½lb onions, sliced	*1½lb onions, sliced*
25g/1oz butter	*2 tablespoons butter*
250ml/8fl oz chicken stock	*1 cup chicken stock*
freshly ground black pepper	*freshly ground black pepper*
2 tablespoons double cream	*2 tablespoons heavy cream*
75g/3oz Gruyère, grated	*¾ cup grated Gruyère*
2 tablespoons olive oil	*2 tablespoons olive oil*
Garnish:	**Garnish:**
1 green pepper, sliced	*1 green pepper, sliced*
10 black olives, stoned	*10 pitted ripe olives*

1. To make the pastry, sift the flour and a pinch of salt into a bowl. Dice the butter into the flour and rub in (cut in). Mix to a dough with the water. Roll out the dough on a floured surface and use it to line a buttered 22 cm/8½ inch flan dish or tart pan. Prick the base lightly with a fork and bake blind in a preheated moderately hot oven (200°C/400°F, Gas Mark 6) for about 10 minutes, until the pastry forms a crust.
2. For the filling, sauté the onions in the butter until transparent. Add the stock, salt and pepper and cook until the liquid has evaporated, stirring all the time. Remove the pan from the heat and stir in the cream.
3. Fill the pastry case with the onions. Use the pepper and the olives to garnish the tart attractively.
4. Sprinkle the grated Gruyère and the oil over the tart and bake for 20 minutes.
5. Serve very hot, possibly with a tomato and egg salad.

Tarte à la Tomate
(Tomato Tart)

METRIC/IMPERIAL	AMERICAN
Pastry:	**Pastry:**
200g/7oz plain flour	*1¾ cups all-purpose flour*
salt	*salt*
100g/3½oz butter	*½ cup butter*
3 tablespoons cold water	*3 tablespoons cold water*
Filling:	**Filling:**
750g/1½lb tomatoes	*1½lb tomatoes*
1 large onion, sliced	*1 large onion, sliced*
½ small red chilli, sliced	*½ small red chili, sliced*
1 clove garlic, crushed	*1 clove garlic, crushed*
15g/½oz butter	*1 tablespoon butter*
freshly ground black pepper	*freshly ground black pepper*
onion rings, to garnish	*onion rings, to garnish*

1. For the pastry, sift the flour and a pinch of salt into a bowl. Dice the butter into the flour and rub in (cut in), then mix to a dough with the water. Roll out the dough on a floured surface and use it to line a buttered 22cm/8½ inch flan dish or tart pan. Prick the base lightly with a fork and bake blind in a preheated moderately hot oven (200°C/400°F, Gas Mark 6) for about 10 minutes, until the pastry has begun to form a slight crust.
2. For the filling, skin 500g/1lb of the tomatoes by first plunging them briefly into boiling water. Chop them up very roughly.
3. Fry the sliced onion, chilli, and the garlic in the butter for 1 minute. Add the chopped tomatoes, salt and pepper. Cover and simmer for about 30 minutes until the tomatoes have formed a smooth purée (if the mixture is very runny, remove the lid from the pan to allow the excess liquid to evaporate).
4. Pour this thick purée into the partly cooked pastry case. Slice the remaining tomatoes into thin rings and arrange them over the surface of the tart together with the onion rings.
5. Bake for 20 minutes in the oven. Serve hot or cold.

◁ *Tarte à l'Oignon (left) and Tarte à la Tomate (right)*

Sabine

*With her golden hair and innocent appeal, Sabine had no
difficulty winning herself a protective, Parisien policeman for a husband.
Aware of the dangers on the street, he often pops home at
lunchtime to give her lessons in self-defence.*

Tarte au Fromage
(Cheese Tart)

METRIC/IMPERIAL
Pastry:
200g/7oz plain flour
salt
100g/3½oz butter
3 tablespoons cold water
Filling:
250ml/8fl oz double cream
200g/7oz Gouda, grated
2 eggs, separated, whites stiffly
    whipped
grated nutmeg
freshly chopped parsley
salt
freshly ground black pepper
2 large ripe tomatoes, sliced
chopped fresh parsley, to
    garnish

AMERICAN
Pastry:
1¾ cups all-purpose flour
salt
½ cup butter
3 tablespoons cold water
Filling:
1 cup heavy cream
1¾ cups grated Gouda
2 eggs, separated, whites stiffly
    whipped
grated nutmeg
freshly chopped parsley
salt
freshly ground black pepper
2 large ripe tomatoes, sliced
chopped fresh parsley, to
    garnish

1. To make the pastry, sift the flour and a pinch of salt into a
bowl. Dice the butter into the flour and rub in (cut in), then
mix to a dough with the water. Roll out the dough on a floured
surface and line a 22cm/8½ inch buttered flan dish or tart pan.
Prick the base lightly with a fork and bake blind in a preheated
moderately hot oven (200°C/400°F, Gas Mark 6) for about 10
minutes, until the pastry has begun to form a slight crust.
2. For the filling, mix together the cream and the Gouda
cheese. Add the egg yolks and then the stiffly whipped whites.
Add nutmeg, parsley, salt and pepper to taste.
3. Pour this into the partly cooked pastry case and arrange
rings of tomato on the surface. Salt the tomatoes lightly.
4. Reduce oven temperature to 160°C/325°F, Gas Mark 3.
Bake the tart for between 30 and 40 minutes in the warm
oven. Serve warm and garnished with freshly chopped parsley.
As cheese makes a very rich tart, I suggest that this is
accompanied by a selection of light tasty salads or crudités.

Tarte au Maïs
(Sweetcorn Tart)

METRIC/IMPERIAL
Pastry:
200 g/7oz plain flour
salt
100g/3½oz butter
3 tablespoons cold water
Filling:
2 large Spanish onions,
    chopped
25g/1oz butter
1 × 300 g/10oz can
    sweetcorn, drained
3 large eggs
2 tablespoons milk
1 teaspoon mixed herbs
pinch of garlic salt
freshly ground black pepper

AMERICAN
Pastry:
1¾ cups all-purpose flour
salt
½ cup butter
3 tablespoons cold water
Filling:
2 large Spanish onions,
    chopped
2 tablespoons butter
1 × 10oz can whole kernel
    corn, drained
3 large eggs
2 tablespoons milk
1 teaspoon mixed herbs
pinch of garlic salt
freshly ground black pepper

1. To make the pastry, sift the flour and a pinch of salt into a
bowl. Dice the butter into the flour and rub in (cut in), then
mix to a dough with the water. Roll out the dough on a floured
surface and line a buttered 22cm/8½ inch flan dish or tart pan.
Prick the base lightly with a fork and bake blind in a preheated
moderately hot oven (200°C/400°F, Gas Mark 6) for about 5
minutes, until the pastry has begun to dry.
2. To make the filling, fry the onions in the butter until they
are transparent. Place them in the pastry case. Cover the
onions with the drained sweetcorn (whole kernel corn).
3. Beat together the eggs, milk, mixed herbs, garlic salt and
pepper and pour over the sweetcorn (whole kernel corn).
4. Bake for 30 minutes and serve hot. Sabine suggests that
this refreshing tart may be served with courgettes (zucchini)
that have been cooked in garlic butter and tiny new potatoes.

Tarte au Fromage ▷

Noémie

Noémie and Robert, her English husband, like to celebrate
Christmas Eve in their own way. This means that Noémie presents
an appealing tart rather than mince pies for the fortunate Father
Christmas who comes down the chimney to fill her stocking.

Quiche au Thon et aux Champignons

(Tuna and Mushroom Quiche)

METRIC/IMPERIAL	AMERICAN
Pastry:	*Pastry:*
200g/7oz plain flour	*1¾ cups all-purpose flour*
salt	*salt*
100g/3½oz butter	*½ cup butter*
3 tablespoons cold water	*3 tablespoons cold water*
Filling:	*Filling:*
1 large onion, chopped	*1 large onion, chopped*
1 clove garlic, crushed	*1 clove garlic, crushed*
175g/6oz mushrooms, sliced	*1½ cups sliced mushrooms*
15g/½oz butter	*1 tablespoon butter*
1 × 200g/7oz can of tuna fish	*1 cup tuna fish*
120ml/4fl oz milk	*½ cup milk*
2 eggs	*2 eggs*
2 tablespoons double cream	*2 tablespoons heavy cream*
1 heaped tablespoon chopped parsley	*1 heaped tablespoon chopped parsley*
freshly ground black pepper	*freshly ground black pepper*

1. To make the pastry, sift the flour and a pinch of salt into a bowl. Dice the butter into the flour and rub in (cut in), then mix to a dough with the water. Roll out the dough on a floured surface and line a buttered 22cm/8½ inch flan dish or tart pan. Prick the base lightly with a fork and bake blind in a preheated moderately hot oven (200°C/400°F, Gas Mark 6) for about 10 minutes, until the pastry has begun to form a slight crust.
2. For the filling, fry the onion, garlic and sliced mushrooms in the butter for 3 to 5 minutes.
3. Drain the tuna and scatter the flakes evenly over the pastry. Cover this with a layer of onion and mushrooms.
4. Beat together the milk, eggs, cream and parsley and add salt and pepper to taste. Pour this in the pastry case.
5. Bake for 30 minutes. Serve hot or cold.

◁ *Tarte au Poulet et aux Poivrons*

Tarte au Poulet et aux Poivrons

(Chicken and Pepper Tart)

METRIC/IMPERIAL	AMERICAN
Pastry:	*Pastry:*
200g/7oz plain flour	*1¾ cups all-purpose flour*
salt	*salt*
100g/3½oz butter	*½ cup butter*
3 tablespoons cold water	*3 tablespoons cold water*
Filling:	*Filling:*
1 medium onion, sliced	*1 medium onion, sliced*
1 clove garlic, crushed	*1 clove garlic, crushed*
15g/½oz butter	*1 tablespoon butter*
500g/1lb cooked chicken	*1lb cooked chicken*
1 small red pepper, sliced	*1 small red pepper, sliced*
1 small green pepper, sliced	*1 small green pepper, sliced*
1 tablespoon tomato purée	*1 tablespoon tomato paste*
1 egg	*1 egg*
120ml/4fl oz double cream	*½ cup heavy cream*
½ teaspoon dried thyme	*½ teaspoon dried thyme*
1 tablespoon fresh parsley	*1 tablespoon fresh parsley*
freshly ground black pepper	*freshly ground black pepper*

1. Sift the flour and a pinch of salt into a bowl. Dice the butter into the flour and rub in (cut in), then mix to a dough with the water. Roll out the dough on a floured surface and use it to line a buttered 22cm/8½ inch flan dish or tart pan. Prick the base lightly with a fork and bake blind in a preheated moderately hot oven (200°C/400°F, Gas Mark 6) for about 10 minutes, until the pastry has begun to form a slight crust.
2. For the filling, fry the onion and garlic in the butter over a medium heat until it begins to soften. Break the chicken into bite-sized pieces and add them to the pan. When the chicken begins to colour add the peppers and cook for a further minute. Stir in the tomato purée (paste).
3. Beat together the egg and the cream with the herbs and salt and pepper to taste. Stir in the chicken and fill the case.
4. Return to the oven for 30 minutes until the filling has set.
5. Serve hot with vegetables for a satisfying main course.

Corinne

*The enterprising manageress of a fish restaurant, Corinne does not
need the lure of aphrodisiac oysters to tempt in her customers.
Her fish tarts, pink, mouth-watering langoustines — and charming,
helpful daughters are temptation enough.*

Tartelettes aux Moules
(Mussel Tartlets)

METRIC/IMPERIAL	AMERICAN
200g/7oz packet frozen puff pastry.	7oz packet frozen puff pastry
1·5 litres/2½ pints fresh mussels	6¼ cups fresh mussels
75g/3oz butter	⅓ cup butter
2 shallots or small strong onions, chopped	2 shallots or small strong onions, chopped
1 clove garlic, crushed	1 clove garlic, crushed
200ml/⅓ pint water	⅞ cup water
7 tablespoons dry white wine	7 tablespoons dry white wine
25g/1oz parsley, freshly chopped	¾ cup parsley, freshly chopped
salt	salt
freshly ground black pepper	freshly ground black pepper
25g/1oz plain flour	¼ cup all-purpose flour
2 egg yolks	2 egg yolks
200 ml/⅓ pint double cream	⅞ cup double cream
chopped parsley, to garnish	chopped parsley, to garnish

1. Defrost and roll out the pastry on a floured board. Butter 6 to 8 tartlet tins and line them with the pastry. (If you have no tartlet tins then bun tins or muffin pans make a good substitute.) Prick the bases with a fork and bake blind in a preheated hot oven (220°C/425°F, Gas Mark 7) for 10 to 12 minutes. Remove the foil and weights from the pastry cases and return to the oven for a further 3 minutes.
2. Scrape and wash the mussels. Melt 40g/1½oz butter in a large heavy based pan and fry the shallots and garlic briskly for 1 minute. Add the mussels, water, wine, parsley, salt and pepper and bring to the boil for about 10 minutes, until the mussels open. Drain the mussels and keep the strained juice to one side.
3. Melt the remaining butter in a small pan and stir in the flour with a wooden spoon to make a roux. Gradually stir in 300ml/½ pint (1¼ cups) of the mussel juice, bring to the boil

and cook until it thickens, stirring all the time. Quickly beat in the egg yolks and continue to cook until it thickens further.
4. Remove the pan from the heat and whisk in the cream, salt and pepper to taste.
5. Remove the mussels from their shells and divide them between the pastry cases. Pour over the sauce and then place the tartlets under a preheated grill (broiler) for a minute or two in order to heat them through. Garnish with fresh parsley.

Flan au Crabe
(Crab Flan)

METRIC/IMPERIAL	AMERICAN
4 eggs	4 eggs
7 tablespoons double cream	7 tablespoons heavy cream
200g/8oz crab meat	1 cup crab meat
pinch of paprika	pinch of paprika
salt	salt
freshly ground black pepper	freshly ground black pepper
1 tablespoon fresh chopped parsley	1 tablespoon fresh chopped parsley
7 tablespoons milk	7 tablespoons milk
Garnish:	**Garnish:**
1 sliced lemon	1 sliced lemon
parsley sprigs	parsley sprigs

1. Beat the eggs in a large bowl then, using a fork, stir in the cream, crab meat, a pinch of paprika, salt, pepper and parsley.
2. Boil the milk. Remove from the heat, leave for a minute then gradually stir it into the crab mixture.
3. Butter a shallow 20cm/8 inch dish and pour in the mixture. Place this dish in a larger dish of water, making a *bain-marie*, and bake in a preheated moderately hot oven (190°C/375°F, Gas Mark 5) for 45 minutes until set.
4. After it has cooled for about 5 minutes, unmould the flan and leave it to cool. Decorate with lemon slices and parsley.

Tartelettes aux Moules (left) and Flan au Crabe (right) ▷

Hyacinthe

Hyacinthe left home and country and found herself a husband in Basildon. Naturally, she lost no time in whisking him back across the Channel in her trusty Deux Chevaux. They often take picnics to deserted beaches, where they relish the joys of uninhibited exploration.

Quiche Provençale

METRIC/IMPERIAL	AMERICAN
Pastry:	**Pastry:**
200g/7oz plain flour	1¾ cups all-purpose flour
salt	salt
100g/3½oz butter	½ cup butter
3 tablespoons cold water	3 tablespoons cold water
Filling:	**Filling:**
2 teaspoons cooking oil	2 teaspoons cooking oil
1 medium onion, sliced	1 medium onion, sliced
200g/7oz aubergine, diced	1¾ cups diced eggplant
200g/7oz courgettes, sliced	1¾ cups sliced zucchini
2 cloves garlic, crushed	2 cloves garlic, crushed
1 red pepper, sliced	1 red pepper, sliced
¼ teaspoon marjoram	¼ teaspoon marjoram
¼ teaspoon thyme	¼ teaspoon thyme
1 teaspoon parsley, freshly chopped	1 teaspoon parsley, freshly chopped
freshly ground black pepper	freshly ground black pepper
2 eggs	2 eggs
120ml/4fl oz cream	½ cup cream
75g/3oz grated Parmesan	¾ cup grated Parmesan

1. To make the pastry, sift the flour and a pinch of salt into a bowl. Dice the butter into the flour and rub in (cut in). Mix to a dough with the water. Roll out the dough on a floured surface and line a buttered 22cm/8½ inch flan dish or tart pan.
2. For the filling, heat the oil in a saucepan. Fry the onion and then the aubergine (eggplant), courgettes (zucchini), garlic and red pepper. Add the herbs, salt and pepper. Stir well and cook gently until soft.
3. In a large bowl beat together the eggs, cream and Parmesan. Remove the vegetables from the pan with a slotted spoon and fold them into the egg mixture. Pour this slowly into the unbaked pastry case and bake in a preheated moderately hot oven (200°C/400°F, Gas Mark 6) for 30 minutes until set.

◁ *Quiche Provençale*

Tarte Pissaladière

METRIC/IMPERIAL	AMERICAN
Pastry:	**Pastry:**
200g/7oz plain flour	1¾ cups all-purpose flour
salt	salt
100g/3½oz butter	½ cup butter
1 egg yolk, beaten	1 egg yolk, beaten
2 tablespoons cold water	2 tablespoons cold water
Filling:	**Filling:**
500g/1lb tomatoes, peeled and chopped	1lb tomatoes, skinned and chopped
1 large onion, chopped	1 large onion, chopped
1 tablespoon oil	1 tablespoon oil
1 clove garlic, crushed	1 clove garlic, crushed
1 bay leaf, crushed	1 bay leaf, crushed
¼ teaspoon thyme	¼ teaspoon thyme
¼ teaspoon oregano	¼ teaspoon oregano
freshly ground black pepper	freshly ground black pepper
2 eggs, beaten	2 eggs, beaten
100g/3½oz Jarlsberg cheese, grated	1 cup grated Jarlsberg cheese
Garnish:	**Garnish:**
1 × 60g/2oz can anchovies	1 × 2oz can anchovies
10 black olives, stoned	10 pitted ripe olives

1. To make the pastry, sift the flour and a pinch of salt into a bowl. Dice the butter into the flour and rub in (cut in). Stir in the beaten egg yolk with a fork. Mix to a dough with the water. Roll out the dough on a floured surface and use it to line a buttered 22cm/8½ inch flan dish or tart pan. Prick the base lightly with a fork and bake blind in a preheated moderately hot oven (200°C/400°F, Gas Mark 6) for about 10 minutes.
2. For the filling, fry the onion in the oil. Add the garlic, tomatoes, herbs, salt and pepper. Cook over a low heat for 20 to 30 minutes, stirring occasionally. Remove from the heat and add eggs and cheese. Pour into the pastry case and garnish with anchovies and olives. Return to the oven and bake for 30 minutes.

Sylvie

Sylvie met her husband Jean-Louis at the Folies Bergères, where he was mesmerized by her performance. Even after five years of marriage the novelty hasn't worn off, and she still performs for him twice nightly.

Tartelettes aux Crevettes
(Prawn Tartlets)

METRIC/IMPERIAL	AMERICAN
Pastry:	**Pastry:**
200g/7oz plain flour	1¾ cups all-purpose flour
salt	salt
100g/3½oz butter	½ cup butter
3 tablespoons cold water	3 tablespoons cold water
Filling:	**Filling:**
1 medium onion, sliced	1 medium onion, sliced
15g/½oz butter	1 tablespoon butter
250g/8oz peeled prawns	1¼ cups shelled shrimp
1 egg, beaten	1 egg, beaten
100g/3½oz fromage blanc (or an unbeaten cream cheese)	½ cup fromage blanc (or an unbeaten cream cheese)
2 tablespoons double cream	2 tablespoons heavy cream
2 teaspoons chopped fresh parsley	2 teaspoons chopped fresh parsley
freshly ground black pepper	freshly ground black pepper
50g/2oz unpeeled prawns to garnish	¼ cup unshelled shrimp to garnish

1. To make the pastry, sift the flour and a pinch of salt into a bowl. Dice the butter into the flour and rub in (cut in), then mix to a dough with the water. Roll out the dough on a floured surface and line buttered individual tartlet tins. Prick the bases lightly with a fork and bake blind in a preheated moderately hot oven (200°C/400°F, Gas Mark 6) for about 5 minutes, until the pastry has begun to form a slight crust.
2. To make the filling, fry the onion in the butter for about 3 minutes. Remove the pan from the heat.
3. Stir in the peeled prawns (shelled shrimp), egg, *fromage blanc*, cream and the parsley and salt and pepper to taste, reserving some chopped parsley to garnish the cooked tartlets.
4. Spoon the filling into the pastry cases, reduce the oven temperature to 180°C/350°F, Gas Mark 4, and bake for 15 to 20 minutes until the filling has set and is a pale gold.
5. Garnish the tartlets with the unpeeled prawns (unshelled shrimp), and sprinkle with the reserved chopped parsley.

Tarte aux Noix
(Walnut Tart)

METRIC/IMPERIAL	AMERICAN
Pastry:	**Pastry:**
200g/7oz wholewheat flour	1¾ cups wholewheat flour
salt	salt
100g/3½oz butter	½ cup butter
3 tablespoons cold water	3 tablespoons cold water
Filling:	**Filling:**
1 large onion, sliced	1 large onion, sliced
1 medium red pepper, chopped	1 medium red pepper, chopped
40g/1½oz butter	3 tablespoons butter
2 eggs	2 eggs
150ml/¼ pint milk	⅔ cup milk
1 teaspoon yeast extract	1 teaspoon yeast extract
freshly ground black pepper	freshly ground black pepper
100g/3½oz walnuts, chopped	1 cup walnuts, chopped
4–8 walnut halves to garnish	4–8 walnut halves to garnish

1. Sift the flour and a pinch of salt into a bowl. Dice the butter into the flour and rub in (cut in), then mix to a dough with the water. Roll out the dough on a floured surface and use it to line a buttered 22cm/8½ inch flan dish or tart pan. Prick the base lightly with a fork and bake blind in a preheated moderately hot oven (200°C/400°F, Gas Mark 6) for about 10 minutes, until the pastry has begun to form a slight crust.
2. To make the filling, fry the onion and pepper in the butter for 3 to 5 minutes.
3. Beat together the eggs, milk, yeast extract and season to taste.
4. Place the onion and pepper in the pastry case. Sprinkle over the chopped walnuts and pour over the eggs and milk.
5. Reduce the oven temperature to 180°C/350°F, Gas Mark 4, and bake for 30 minutes until the filling has set.
6. Garnish the cooked tart with the walnut halves.

Tartelettes aux Crevettes ▷

Escorts...
a bit on the side

The well-turned out tart is rarely seen without an escort.
Savoury tarts will always enjoy the company of a crisp
salad, however dressed. And sweet tarts will appreciate
something rich and complementary.

Dressing

The dressing you choose should always enhance the salad. Don't feel tied to vinaigrette — experiment with fresh herbs, mayonnaise and yogurt.

Vinaigrette Facile

(Simple Vinaigrette)

METRIC/IMPERIAL	AMERICAN
3 tablespoons wine vinegar	3 tablespoons wine vinegar
6 tablespoons vegetable oil	6 tablespoons vegetable oil
1 crushed garlic clove	1 crushed garlic clove
pinch salt	pinch salt
freshly ground black pepper	freshly ground black pepper
pinch sugar	pinch sugar
½ teaspoon dried herbs of your choice	½ teaspoon dried herbs of your choice

Shake the ingredients together in a screw-top jar. Store in a cool place and use to dress any fresh salad. Makes about 120ml/4fl oz (½ cup).

Sauce Piquante

(Piquant Sauce)

METRIC/IMPERIAL	AMERICAN
6 tablespoons tomato juice	6 tablespoons tomato juice
2 tablespoons lemon juice	2 tablespoons lemon juice
1 teaspoon Worcestershire sauce	1 teaspoon Worcestershire sauce
1 tablespoon chopped fresh parsley	1 tablespoon chopped fresh parsley
salt	salt
freshly ground black pepper	freshly ground black pepper

Mix together the ingredients in a screw-top jar. Cover and shake well. Taste and adjust the seasonings if necessary. Store in the refrigerator.

Vinaigrette de Coriandre

(Coriander Dressing)

Coriander is similar to flat-leafed parsley but it has a very strong, oriental flavour. This dressing is especially nice on a mixed salad of chopped raw white cabbage, lettuce, cucumber and tomato.

METRIC/IMPERIAL	AMERICAN
6 tablespoons corn, sunflower or olive oil	6 tablespoons corn, sunflower or olive oil
4 tablespoons white vinegar	4 tablespoons white vinegar
½ teaspoon mustard	½ teaspoon mustard
2 teaspoons lemon juice	2 teaspoons lemon juice
2 tablespoons chopped fresh coriander	2 tablespoons chopped fresh coriander
salt	salt
freshly ground black pepper	freshly ground black pepper

Shake together all the ingredients in a screw-top jar. Taste and adjust the seasoning if necessary. Store in a cool place. Makes about 200ml/⅓ pint (⅞ cup).

Vinaigrette de Renée

(Renée's Vinaigrette)

METRIC/IMPERIAL	AMERICAN
4 tablespoons sunflower oil	4 tablespoons sunflower oil
1½ tablespoons white wine vinegar	1½ tablespoons white wine vinegar
1 clove garlic, finely chopped	1 clove garlic, finely chopped
1 shallot, finely chopped	1 shallot, finely chopped
1 tablespoon chopped fresh parsley	1 tablespoon chopped fresh parsley
salt	salt
freshly ground black pepper	freshly ground black pepper
½ teaspoon French mustard	½ teaspoon Dijon-style mustard

Place all the ingredients in a screw top jar. Stir or shake well before serving. This vinaigrette will keep well if stored, covered, in the refrigerator. Makes about 6 tablespoons.

Vinaigrette de Coriandre ▷

Mayonnaise de Daphne
(Daphne's Mayonnaise)

METRIC/IMPERIAL	AMERICAN
2 egg yolks (room temperature)	2 egg yolks (room temperature)
½ teaspoon mustard powder	½ teaspoon mustard powder
salt	salt
freshly ground black pepper	freshly ground black pepper
300ml/½ pint vegetable oil	1¼ cups vegetable oil
1 tablespoon white wine vinegar	1 tablespoon white wine vinegar

1. Place the egg yolks, mustard powder, salt and pepper in a large, cool bowl and whisk them together with a balloon whisk.
2. Slowly whisk in the oil, drop by drop. The oil should be at room temperature. The mayonnaise will begin to thicken.
3. When you have added half of the oil stir in the vinegar. Then continue to whisk in the remaining oil, a little faster this time. The mayonnaise should now be thick, pale and creamy. Adjust the seasoning if necessary and keep in the refrigerator before serving.

Lemon Mayonnaise
This is made in exactly the same way as Daphne's mayonnaise, only lemon juice is substituted for the wine vinegar. Grated lemon rind may be added to enhance the flavour. This mayonnaise is especially delicious with chicken tart (see page 69) or a green salad.

Sauce Aïoli
(Garlic Mayonnaise)

Although this is not the sauce to eat before a romantic assignation, it is especially nice with a meaty tart or to spice up fresh raw vegetables.

METRIC/IMPERIAL	AMERICAN
2 egg yolks	2 egg yolks
4 cloves garlic, crushed	4 cloves garlic, crushed
300ml/½ pint olive oil	1¼ cups olive oil
1 tablespoon lemon juice	1 tablespoon lemon juice
salt	salt
freshly ground black pepper	freshly ground black pepper

1. Whisk the egg yolks with a fork in a cool bowl.
2. Blend the garlic with 1 tablespoon of the olive oil. Beat this into the yolks.
3. Slowly, drop by drop, whisk in the remaining oil until the aïoli is thick and creamy.
4. Stir in the lemon juice and salt and pepper to taste. Store in the refrigerator.

Mayonnaise Minceur
(Slimmer's Dressing)

METRIC/IMPERIAL	AMERICAN
150ml/¼ pint plain yogurt	⅔ cup plain yogurt
1½ tablespoons lemon juice	1½ tablespoons lemon juice
1 tablespoon chopped fresh parsley	1 tablespoon chopped fresh parsley
1 tablespoon chopped fresh chives	1 tablespoon chopped fresh chives
1 tablespoon chopped fresh mint	1 tablespoon chopped fresh mint
salt	salt
freshly ground black pepper	freshly ground black pepper

Place all the ingredients in a screw-top jar, cover and shake well. Store in a cool place and use as a virtuous alternative to richer salad dressings. Makes about 200ml/⅓ pint (⅞ cup).

◁ *Mayonnaise Minceur*

81

Something Sweet

*As well as the traditional English sweet toppings of custard or cream, try
fruit or jam sauces or flavoured ice creams to accompany sweet tarts.*

Sauce à la Confiture
(Jam Sauce)

METRIC/IMPERIAL	AMERICAN
4 tablespoons jam (use a flavour that will complement the tart)	4 tablespoons jam (use a flavor that will complement the tart)
150ml/¼ pint water	⅔ cup water
1 teaspoon cornflour	1 teaspoon cornstarch
1 teaspoon lemon juice	1 teaspoon lemon juice

1. Bring the jam and water to the boil, stir well, lower the heat and simmer for 2 minutes. Remove from the heat.
2. Mix the cornflour (cornstarch) to a paste with a little water. Add to the jam and stir well. Return the sauce to the heat and bring to the boil. Stir in the lemon juice and serve.

Glace à la Vanille
(Vanilla Ice Cream)

METRIC/IMPERIAL	AMERICAN
600ml/1 pint milk	2½ cups milk
1 vanilla pod	1 vanilla bean
4 egg yolks	4 egg yolks
100g/3½oz caster sugar	scant ½ cup sugar
300ml/½ pint thick cream	1¼ cups heavy cream

1. Bring the milk to the boil in a small saucepan with the vanilla pod (bean). Leave to cool slightly for about 10 minutes and discard the pod.
2. Whisk together the yolks and sugar in a medium bowl until light and frothy. Whisk in the milk. Return to a low heat in the saucepan and bring to just below boiling point until it has thickened (do not allow it to boil), stirring all the time with a wooden spoon. Set aside to cool completely.
3. Whip the cream until it is thick, then fold into the milk and egg mixture. Place in a small freezing container and freeze for at least 8 hours. Remove the ice cream from the freezer half an hour before serving in order to soften it. This recipe can be made in double quantity without impairing the flavour.

Sauce à la Fraise
(Strawberry Sauce)

This sauce may be frozen and served as a very light ice cream.

METRIC/IMPERIAL	AMERICAN
300ml/½ pint double cream	1¼ cups heavy cream
6 tablespoons caster sugar	6 tablespoons sugar
750g/1½lb strawberries	1½lb strawberries
4 egg whites	4 egg whites

1. Whip the cream lightly.
2. Using a food processor or blender, purée together the sugar and the strawberries. Fold into the cream.
3. Whisk the egg whites until stiff and fold them into the strawberry cream. Chill and serve as an unusual frothy strawberry sauce.

Crème Anglaise
(Real English Custard)

METRIC/IMPERIAL	AMERICAN
2 egg yolks	2 egg yolks
1 heaped tablespoon caster sugar	1 heaped tablespoon sugar
300ml/½ pint milk	1¼ cups milk
vanilla essence	vanilla

1. Beat the yolks with a fork and whisk in the sugar until mixture is pale.
2. Bring the milk and a few drops of vanilla slowly to the boil in a medium saucepan. Pour this onto the yolks, stir well and return the mixture to the pan. Stir over a moderate heat until the custard has thickened. Serve hot or cold as a creamy partner for any fruit tart. Alternatively, freeze and serve as an ice cream

Sauce à la Fraise ▷

Glace aux Abricots

(Apricot Ice Cream)

METRIC/IMPERIAL	AMERICAN
500g/1lb apricots, stoned	1lb apricots, pitted
75g/3oz sugar	6 tablespoons sugar
150ml/¼ pint water	⅔ cup water
150ml/¼ pint double cream, whipped	⅔ cup heavy cream, whipped
6 tablespoons apricot jam, sieved	6 tablespoons apricot jam, sieved

1. Poach the apricots with the sugar and water until they are tender. Purée them in a blender or food processor and leave to cool.
2. Fold the whipped cream into the apricot purée. Freeze until almost solid, about 2 to 4 hours. Remove from the freezer and whisk to beat out any ice crystals.
3. Warm the sieved apricot jam in a small pan, then stir this into the fruit and cream so that a 'ripple' effect is obtained. Refreeze for about 8 hours. Serve with an apricot tart.

Glace au Citron

(Lemon Ice Cream)

METRIC/IMPERIAL	AMERICAN
2 lemons	2 lemons
300ml/½ pint double cream	1¼ cups heavy cream
2 eggs	2 eggs
2 tablespoons caster sugar	2 tablespoons sugar
300ml/½ pint milk	1¼ cups milk

1. Finely grate the rind of the lemons, then squeeze the juice. Beat the rind and juice with the cream. Beat in the eggs, and stir in the sugar and milk. Mix well.
2. Freeze for a minimum of 8 hours. Remove from the freezer at least 30 minutes before serving to allow the ice cream to soften slightly.

◁ *Glace aux Abricots*

Glace au Chocolat

(Chocolate Ice Cream)

METRIC/IMPERIAL	AMERICAN
300ml/½ pint milk	1¼ cups milk
125g/4oz plain chocolate	4 squares semi-sweet chocolate
1 teaspoon instant coffee granules	1 teaspoon instant coffee granules
4 egg yolks	4 egg yolks
75g/3oz sugar	6 tablespoons sugar
150ml/¼ pint double cream	⅔ cup heavy cream

1. Scald the milk by bringing it just to the boil, then remove the pan from the heat. Add the chocolate pieces and the coffee granules. Leave until the chocolate has melted completely, about 10 minutes. Stir.
2. In a medium bowl whisk the yolks and sugar until pale and frothy. Whisk in the milk, pour the mixture into the pan and return it to a low heat. Whisk over the heat until it thickens, do not boil the mixture. Cool completely. Whip the cream until stiff and fold it into the chocolate mixture. Freeze for at least 8 hours. Just before it is quite frozen, beat with a fork to break up any ice crystals.

Sorbet de Fruits Doux

(Soft Fruit Sorbet)

This sorbet may be made with any soft fruit. I particularly enjoy blackcurrant sorbet, sprinkled with Cassis liqueur. However, strawberries, raspberries, gooseberries and blackberries all make delicious, refreshing sorbets.

Fruit purée is simple to make: place about 500g/1lb of prepared fruit in a pan with 2 tablespoons water and poach briefly until tender. Sieve to give a smooth purée.

METRIC/IMPERIAL	AMERICAN
200g/7oz sugar	1 cup sugar
600ml/1 pint water	2½ cups water
600ml/1 pint fruit purée	2½ cups fruit purée

1. Heat the sugar with the water until it has dissolved.
2. Cool the syrup then bring to the boil and boil until the mixture is syrupy. Mix in the fruit purée. Stir well.
3. Freeze the sorbet for at least 8 hours – just before it is completely solid, beat it with a fork to remove ice crystals.

Salads

When you make a salad, you can be as creative as you wish. Mix together a variety of ingredients to produce something really colourful.

Ratatouille Froide
(Cold Ratatouille)

METRIC/IMPERIAL
1 large onion, sliced
15g/½oz butter
1 tablespoon cooking oil
500g/1lb courgettes, sliced
125g/4oz aubergine, chopped
1 × 250g/8oz can tomatoes
1 large clove garlic, crushed
1 teaspoon dried Herbes de
  Provence (thyme, rosemary
  and bay)
salt
freshly ground black pepper

AMERICAN
1 large onion, sliced
1 tablespoon butter
1 tablespoon cooking oil
1 lb zucchini, sliced
1 cup diced eggplant
1 × 8oz can tomatoes
1 large clove garlic, crushed
1 teaspoon dried Herbes de
  Provence (thyme, rosemary
  and bay)
salt
freshly ground black pepper

1. Lightly fry the onion in the butter and oil over a medium heat for 1 to 2 minutes. Stir in the courgettes (zucchini) and aubergine (eggplant) and mix well with a wooden spoon. Add the tomatoes, garlic, herb and salt and pepper to taste.
2. Bring to the boil and simmer for 15 to 20 minutes until courgettes (zucchini) and aubergine (eggplant) are quite tender. It may be necessary to add a little extra water during cooking.
3. Chill the ratatouille well and serve with a savoury tart.

Salade de Crabe
(Crab Salad)

METRIC/IMPERIAL
2 ripe avocados
1 tablespoon lemon juice
125g/4oz crab meat
50g/2oz walnuts
2 celery sticks, chopped
4–6 tablespoons Sauce
  Piquante (see page 78)
paprika

AMERICAN
2 ripe avocados
1 tablespoon lemon juice
4oz crab meat
½ cup walnuts
2 celery stalks, chopped
4–6 tablespoons Sauce
  Piquante (see page 78)
paprika

To serve:
4–6 lettuce leaves
4–6 crab or scallop shells
  (optional)
lemon slices
fresh parsley sprigs

To serve:
4–6 lettuce leaves
4–6 crab or scallop shells
  (optional)
lemon slices
fresh parsley sprigs

1. Peel and chop the avocados. Toss in the lemon juice and stir in the crab, walnuts and celery.
2. To serve, place a lettuce leaf in each of the crab or scallop shells or in individual dishes. Divide the avocado and crab mixture between them.
3. Pour a tablespoon of Sauce Piquante over each serving and sprinkle with paprika. Garnish with lemon slices and fresh parsley and serve.

Betterave à l'Orange
(Beetroot with Orange)

METRIC/IMPERIAL
500g/1lb cooked beetroot,
  peeled and sliced
1 teaspoon plain flour
25g/1oz soft brown sugar
150ml/¼ pint fresh orange
  juice
1 tablespoon wine vinegar
salt
freshly ground black pepper
25g/1oz butter

AMERICAN
1lb cooked beet, peeled and
  sliced
1 teaspoon all-purpose flour
1½ tablespoons light brown
  sugar
⅔ cup fresh orange juice
1 tablespoon wine vinegar
salt
freshly ground black pepper
2 tablespoons butter

1. Place the beetroot in an ovenproof dish.
2. Mix together the flour and sugar. Slowly stir in the orange juice and vinegar, season with salt and pepper and pour over the beetroot. Dot the surface with the butter.
3. Bake in a preheated moderate oven (180°C/350°F, Gas Mark 4) for 15 minutes. Serve cold.

Salade de Crabe ▷

Concombre à la Crème
(Cucumber with Cream)

METRIC/IMPERIAL	AMERICAN
1 cucumber, peeled and sliced	1 cucumber, peeled and sliced
4 tablespoons double cream	4 tablespoons heavy cream
salt	salt
freshly ground black pepper	freshly ground black pepper
1 tablespoon chopped fresh mint	1 tablespoon chopped fresh mint

1. Mix together the cucumber slices, cream, salt and pepper.
2. Arrange the cucumber on a flat dish and sprinkle it with the mint. Chill the salad and serve.

Salade de Tous les Jours
(Everyday Salad)

METRIC/IMPERIAL	AMERICAN
a selection of any of the following salad greens – Cos lettuce, Webbs lettuce, curly endive; **or** 2 heads of chicory, sliced; **or** 1 small white cabbage, sliced	a selection of any of the following salad greens – romaine lettuce, iceberg lettuce, chicory; **or** 2 heads of endive, sliced; **or** 1 small white cabbage, sliced
4–6 tablespoons Renée's vinaigrette (see page 78)	4–6 tablespoons Renée's vinaigrette (see page 78)

Wash and prepare the selected salad greens. Dry thoroughly using a salad spinner or by swinging it around your head in a tea towel or blanching basket. Toss thoroughly in Renée's vinaigrette and serve at once.

Salade aux Herbes Fraîches
(Fresh Herb Salad)

Collect a few leaves or sprigs of as many herbs as you can. Christine who invented this salad gathers from her garden three pieces of the following: lemon balm, thyme, basil, parsley, chives, chickweed, chervil, salad Burnett and sorrel.

METRIC/IMPERIAL	AMERICAN
1 flat-leafed lettuce	1 flat-leafed lettuce
a selection of fresh herbs (see above)	a selection of fresh herbs (see above)
4–6 tablespoons Renée's vinaigrette (see page 78)	4–6 tablespoons Renée's vinaigrette (see page 78)
borage flowers or rose petals to garnish	borage flowers or rose petals to garnish

1. Wash the lettuce and dry well. Wash the herbs and dry them thoroughly between two pieces of absorbent kitchen paper.
2. Break the herbs into small, decorative pieces with your fingers.
3. Toss the lettuce in the vinaigrette with the herbs until well coated. Sprinkle the borage or rose petals over the salad and serve.

Carottes Rapées
(Grated Carrot)

METRIC/IMPERIAL	AMERICAN
500g/1lb carrots, grated	1lb carrots, grated
120ml/4fl oz Renée's vinaigrette (see page 78)	½ cup Renée's vinaigrette (see page 78)
4 to 6 lettuce leaves	4 to 6 lettuce leaves
1 tablespoon chopped fresh parsley to garnish	1 tablespoon chopped fresh parsley to garnish

1. Mix the freshly grated carrot with the vinaigrette in a large bowl. Stir well to coat the carrot thoroughly with the dressing and adjust the seasoning if necessary.
2. Arrange the lettuce leaves on a flat dish or shallow bowl and cover with the grated carrot. Sprinkle with the chopped parsley. Chill and serve.

◁ Salade aux Herbes Fraîches

Salade d'Haricots Verts

(French Bean Salad)

Coarsely chopped tomatoes may be used as a substitute for the tuna in this recipe.

METRIC/IMPERIAL	AMERICAN
500g/1lb French beans, cooked and cooled	1lb green beans, cooked and cooled
75g/3oz tuna fish	½ cup tuna fish
4 tablespoons Renée's vinaigrette (see page 78)	4 tablespoons Renée's vinaigrette (see page 78)
1 small onion, chopped	1 small onion, chopped
1 clove garlic, finely chopped	1 clove garlic, finely chopped
1 tablespoon chopped fresh parsley	1 tablespoon chopped fresh parsley
salt	salt
freshly ground black pepper	freshly ground black pepper

1. Stir together the beans, tuna and vinaigrette. Transfer to a shallow dish.
2. Mix together the onion, garlic and parsley and sprinkle evenly over the beans. Season to taste with salt and pepper. Chill and serve.

Couronne de Riz

(Rice Crown)

METRIC/IMPERIAL	AMERICAN
250g/8oz long-grain rice, cooked	1 cup long-grain rice, cooked
½ small red pepper, diced	½ small red pepper, diced
½ small cucumber, diced	½ small cucumber, diced
150g/5oz tuna fish	⅔ cup tuna fish
4–6 tablespoons Renée's vinaigrette (see page 78)	4–6 tablespoons Renée's vinaigrette (see page 78)
freshly ground black pepper	freshly ground black pepper
2 medium tomatoes	2 medium tomatoes
6 black olives, halved and stoned	6 pitted ripe olives, halved
lettuce leaves to garnish	lettuce leaves to garnish

1. Stir together the rice, pepper, cucumber, tuna fish and enough vinaigrette to coat every grain of rice. Add extra pepper, to taste, if necessary.

2. Chop one tomato and mix with the rice. Cut the remaining tomato in half lengthwise and remove the core and pips. Slice the flesh into narrow strips.
3. Lightly butter a ring mould. Place the olives and strips of tomato in a pattern around the base. Fill the mould with the rice salad; press it down firmly and chill.
4. To serve, unmould the rice crown onto a round plate and fill the centre with lettuce leaves.

Salade aux Pâtes

(Pasta Salad)

METRIC/IMPERIAL	AMERICAN
500g/1lb garlic sausage, diced	2 cups diced garlic sausage
175g/6oz pasta shells, cooked	1½ cups pasta shells, cooked
125g/4oz button mushrooms, halved	1 cup button mushrooms, halved
1 small red pepper, thinly sliced	1 small red pepper, thinly sliced
1 small onion, finely chopped	1 small onion, finely chopped
8 black olives, halved and stoned	8 pitted ripe olives, halved
2 tablespoons red wine vinegar	2 tablespoons red wine vinegar
6 tablespoons olive oil	6 tablespoons olive oil
1 tablespoon tomato purée	1 tablespoon tomato paste
1 teaspoon dried mixed herbs	1 teaspoon dried mixed herbs
salt	salt
freshly ground black pepper	freshly ground black pepper
1 tablespoon chopped fresh parsley to garnish	1 tablespoon chopped fresh parsley to garnish

1. Mix the garlic sausage and the pasta. Add the mushrooms, pepper, onion and olives.
2. Blend together the vinegar, olive oil, tomato purée (paste) and mixed herbs. Add salt and pepper to taste.
3. Stir well into the pasta mixture. Sprinkle with parsley, chill and serve.

Salade aux Pâtes (top) and Couronne de Riz (below) ▷

Crudités Marinées

(Marinated Celery, Carrot and Sweet Pepper Strips)

These crudités are an original appetizer to serve with aperitifs or make an unusual addition to a side salad.

METRIC/IMPERIAL	AMERICAN
4 large carrots	4 large carrots
4 celery sticks	4 celery stalks
3 large peppers, green, red and yellow	3 large peppers, green, red and yellow
300ml/½ pint Renée's vinaigrette (see page 78)	1¼ cups Renée's vinaigrette (see page 78)
Garnish:	*Garnish:*
2 tablespoons chopped fresh parsley	2 tablespoons chopped fresh parsley
freshly ground black pepper	freshly ground black pepper

1. Wash and peel the carrots, then cut them into julienne (matchstick-like) strips. Cover with a third of the vinaigrette.
2. Wash and cut the celery into julienne (matchstick-like) strips. Cover with the second third of the vinaigrette.
3. Wash the pepper. Remove the seeds and slice thinly lengthways. Cover in the remaining vinaigrette. Leave the vegetables to marinate overnight in the refrigerator.
4. The next day remove the vegetable strips from their marinades with a slotted spoon. Arrange the strips on a large round plate as though they were the spokes of a wheel. Sprinkle with parsley and pepper, chill if necessary and serve.

Petits Oignons Dentelés

(Frilly Spring Onions)

METRIC/IMPERIAL	AMERICAN
1 bunch spring onions	1 bunch scallions
600ml/1 pint ice cold water	2½ cups ice cold water

1. Wash the onions and trim to 5cm/2 inches above the bulb. Slit the stalk lengthways with a sharp knife two or three times.
2. Place the onions in the cold water and leave in the refrigerator for a few hours. The stems will curl and frill. Drain and use as a striking garnish for any salad or tart.

◁ *Salade Rapide (top left) and Crudités Marinées (below)*

Salade au Cresson

(Watercress Salad)

The flavour of the orange in this salad reduces the bitterness of the watercress and gives the salad a refreshing taste.

METRIC/IMPERIAL	AMERICAN
1 bunch watercress	1 bunch watercress
1 large orange	1 large orange
2 celery sticks, chopped	2 celery stalks, chopped
50g/2oz walnuts	½ cup walnuts
3 tablespoons walnut oil (or olive oil if walnut oil is not available)	3 tablespoons walnut oil (or olive oil if walnut oil is not available)
1 tablespoon red wine vinegar	1 tablespoon red wine vinegar
½ teaspoon French mustard	½ teaspoon Dijon-style mustard
salt	salt
freshly ground black pepper	freshly ground black pepper

1. Wash and dry the watercress and trim away most of the stems. Peel the orange with a sharp knife. Slice it thinly into rounds and then cut the rounds into quarters. Mix the watercress, celery, orange and walnuts together.
2. Blend together the walnut oil, vinegar, mustard, salt and pepper. Toss the salad well in the vinaigrette.

Salade Rapide

(Quick Salad)

When guests turn up unexpectedly, serve this as an easy and fast hors d'oeuvre with a tart as a main course.

METRIC/IMPERIAL	AMERICAN
1 × 425g/15oz can artichoke hearts	1 × 15oz can artichoke hearts
1 × 425g/15oz can coeurs de palmier	1 × 15oz can coeurs de palmier
1 × 425g/15oz can asparagus	1 × 15oz can asparagus
2–3 tablespoons Renée's vinaigrette (see page 78)	2–3 tablespoons Renée's vinaigrette (see page 78)
fresh parsley sprigs to garnish	fresh parsley sprigs to garnish

1. Drain the canned artichokes, palm hearts and asparagus and arrange on a serving dish.
2. Spoon over the vinaigrette and garnish with parsley.

Salade Cauchoise
(Cauchoise Salad)

This version of a potato salad originates from the Caux region of Normandy – Maupassant country, where the ground is flat and the cliffs spectacular.

METRIC/IMPERIAL	AMERICAN
1.75kg/4lb small new potatoes	4lb small new potatoes
1 bunch celery, finely sliced	1 head celery, finely sliced
150ml/¼ pint double cream	⅔ cup heavy cream
1 tablespoon white vinegar	1 tablespoon white vinegar
1 tablespoon lemon juice	1 tablespoon lemon juice
1 tablespoon chopped fresh parsley	1 tablespoon chopped fresh parsley
salt	salt
freshly ground black pepper	freshly ground black pepper
50g/2oz raw ham or bacon, diced	¼ cup diced raw ham or bacon
1 tablespoon chopped fresh chives to garnish	1 tablespoon chopped fresh chives to garnish

1. Wash the potatoes but do not peel. Cook them in a pan of boiling water until tender. Drain and leave them to cool, then peel, using a blunt knife – they should shed their skins easily. (This method of cooking ensures that the potatoes retain maximum flavour and have a buttery texture.) Slice the peeled potatoes into rounds.
2. Mix the potato with the celery, cream, vinegar and lemon juice. Add the parsley and salt and pepper to taste.
3. Add the ham or bacon to the salad; stir well and sprinkle with chives.

Salade aux Pignons de Pin
(Pine Nut Salad)

METRIC/IMPERIAL	AMERICAN
1 radicchio or Cos lettuce	1 head red or romaine lettuce
50g/2oz pine nuts	½ cup pine nuts
4 tablespoons simple vinaigrette (see page 78)	4 tablespoons simple vinaigrette (see page 78)

1. Prepare the lettuce, tearing the large leaves in half.
2. Toss the lettuce, pine nuts and vinaigrette in a large bowl and serve immediately.

Choufleur à la Mayonnaise
(Cauliflower Mayonnaise)

METRIC/IMPERIAL	AMERICAN
250g/8oz cauliflower	½lb cauliflower
1 medium carrot, diced	1 medium carrot, diced
150ml/¼ pint Daphne's mayonnaise (see page 81)	⅔ cup Daphne's mayonnaise (see page 81)
50g/2oz Gruyère cheese, grated	½ cup grated Gruyére cheese
Garnish:	**Garnish:**
chopped fresh parsley	chopped fresh parsley
freshly ground black pepper	freshly ground black pepper

1. Wash the cauliflower and break it into florets the size of a thumbnail. Mix with the diced carrot.
2. Mix Daphne's mayonnaise with the Gruyère cheese. Stir it into the cauliflower and diced carrot.
3. Transfer to a serving dish; sprinkle with parsley and pepper.

Champignons à la Grècque
(Mushrooms à la Grècque)

METRIC/IMPERIAL	AMERICAN
4 tablespoons tomato purée	4 tablespoons tomato paste
250ml/8fl oz water	1 cup water
4 tablespoons corn or olive oil	4 tablespoons corn or olive oil
150ml/¼ pint wine	⅔ cup wine
1 Spanish onion or 2 shallots, chopped	1 Bermuda or Spanish onion or 2 shallots, chopped
1 clove garlic, chopped	1 clove garlic, chopped
8 coriander seeds	8 coriander seeds
¼ teaspoon saffron or 1 teaspoon turmeric	¼ teaspoon saffron or 1 teaspoon turmeric
salt	salt
freshly ground black pepper	freshly ground black pepper
500g/1lb button mushrooms	1lb button mushrooms
chopped parsley to garnish	chopped parsley to garnish

1. Mix the tomato purée (paste), water, oil, wine, onion, garlic, coriander seeds, saffron (or turmeric), salt and pepper in a medium saucepan. Bring to the boil and simmer for 20 minutes. Stir occasionally and add more water if necessary.
2. Wash and trim the mushrooms. Add them to the sauce and simmer for a further 20 minutes. Serve hot or chilled.

INDEX

ACKNOWLEDGMENTS

Photography by Martin Brigdale
Photographic assistants: Steve Hyde and Nick Carman
Food for photography prepared by Jackie Baxter and Jane Suthering
Photographic stylist: Liz Hippisley

The publishers would like to thank the following companies
for the loan of accessories for photography:

Anvil Interiors, 55 New King's Road, SW6; David Mellor, 4 Sloane
Square, London SW1; Divertimenti, 139 Fulham Road, London SW3;
General Trading Company, 144 Sloane Street, London SW1;
Putnam's, 72 Mill Lane, London NW6; Rockingham's Nurseries,
181 Upper Richmond Road, London SW14; Through the Looking Glass,
New King's Road, London SW6.

And special thanks to Alfred Dunhill Limited,
30 Duke Street, St James's, London SW1Y 6DL
for the loan of the watch used on page 20.